HOW-TO BOOK OF
BIRDHOUSES AND FEEDERS

by Paul Meisel

Fox
Chapel Publishing

1970 Broad Street • East Petersburg, PA 17520
www.FoxChapelPublishing.com

Publisher	Alan Giagnocavo
Book Editor	Ayleen Stellhorn
Editorial Assistant	Gretchen Bacon
Cover Design	Jon Deck
Layout and Design	Alan Davis

ISBN 1–56523–237–2
Library of Congress Control Number:
2004106144

To order your copy of this book,
please send check or money order
for the cover price plus $3.50 shipping to:
Fox Chapel Publishing
Book Orders
1970 Broad St.
East Petersburg, PA 17520
1-800-457-9112

Or visit us on the web at **www.FoxChapelPublishing.com**

Manufactured in China

10 9 8 7 6 5 4 3 2 1

Because working with wood inherently includes the risk of injury and damage, this book cannot guarantee that creating the projects in this book is safe for everyone. For this reason, this book is sold without warranties or guarantees of any kind, expressed or implied, and the publisher and author disclaim any liability for any injuries, losses or damages caused in any way by the content of this book or the reader's use of the tools or materials necessary to complete the projects presented here. The publisher and the author urge all woodworkers to thoroughly review each project and to understand the use of all tools and materials involved before beginning any project.

Dedication

I would like to dedicate this book to Harold Doepke, one of the greatest men I have ever had the privilege to work with.

Acknowledgments

Boyd Emerson, Dana Shaw, Sabrina Kraskey, Chris Larsen, Mike Luethmers, Barb Stueve, Kim Truax

Special thanks to Tom Elliott for providing the live bird photography in this book.
(479) 253-0118   telliot@ipa.net

Special thanks to Wild Bird Centers of America, Inc. for providing the feeding preferences in this book.

Wild Bird Centers of America, Inc.
National Headquarters and Training Center
7370 MacArthur Boulevard
Glen Echo, MD 20812
(800) WILDBIRD
info@wildbird.com, www.wildbird.com

Table of Contents

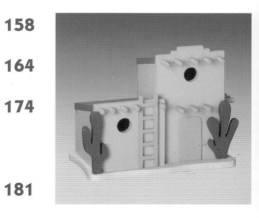

About the Author

Paul Meisel's experience in woodworking and design is extensive. During his ten years as an industrial arts instructor, Mr. Meisel realized the need for project plans that the beginning woodworker could manage. He began designing projects that excited interest in students yet did not exceed their skill level.

Realizing the need for well-designed plans for the school as well as the home-hobbyist woodworker, he and his wife, Pat, set about creating a mail order company for the distribution of these plans. They took their unique concept one step further by offering many hard-to-find specialty hardware parts. This company, Meisel Hardware Specialties, has become one of the nation's leading project plan and woodworking supply companies.

Their company has published plans for over 3,000 woodworking projects, all of which feature Mr. Meisel's rigid criteria for simple, practical construction. He is dedicated to providing fresh ideas that focus on clean, straightforward designs to create maximum impact and that use common lumber sizes and simple painting and finishing techniques. He specifies materials and power tools that are readily available to the do-it-yourselfer.

Mr. Meisel has received numerous awards for his woodworking projects. Many of his designs have appeared in books and magazines. Based in part on his experience as a shop instructor, he has published over 20 booklets in the area of technology education and has also written books on designing and creating board games, on chemical safety and on measurement. In 1993, Mr. Meisel co-authored a book with Patrick Spielman titled *Country Mailboxes*. In 1999, Mr. Meisel's book, *Making Lawn Ornaments in Wood*, was published by Fox Chapel Publishing Company, and in 2002, his book, *The Big Book of Christmas Scroll Saw Projects*, was also published by Fox Chapel Publishing Company.

Part One
Birdhouse Basics

This book is a collection of unique birdhouses and birdfeeders designed for people who want to build objects that are as much yard decorations as they are serious bird-friendly projects. Whether you're looking for something elegant, like the Tylerville Tudor Apartments Birdhouse (see page 104), or something humorous, like the Outhouse Birdhouse (see page 80), you'll find it within the pages of this book.

Birds will not pick a nesting box based solely on bright colors or aesthetic beauty; however, humans do. Therefore, these eye-catching, functional versions are the types of houses and feeders you will see pictured here. Some are bright; some are fun; some are silly, created with only a passing regard to what most would consider an ideal birding structure.

Keep in mind that birds, if given a choice, will, by natural instinct, seek the most inconspicuous hideaways possible. If you are truly concerned about this, I suggest that you paint your birdhouse with dull, flat colors such as gray, brown or green instead of using some of the bright colors that I have chosen.

Now I realize that some of you will want much more than just a pretty addition to your yard. Please rest assured that I have not neglected the needs of birds with these designs. All of these projects will attract some type of bird. If there is a particular bird you wish to attract, it will be necessary for you to be somewhat selective in which birdhouses you choose to make. Entrance hole diameter, cavity size, mounting height and location do play a part in a bird's choice of home. A sampling of these specifics is presented in the Appendix of this book. Additional information is available through field guides and birding books found at your local bookstore or library.

TOOLS AND WOOD

All of the projects in this book are designed to be built in the average home shop. The basic machine tools required are a scroll saw, a table saw and a hand drill or a drill press. A router and a drum sander (or a drum sander attachment for your drill press) are not necessary but will simplify the building process.

Material costs are kept low because only common sizes of lumber and plywood are specified. Where solid lumber is called for, ¾" thick pine boards are specified. Some builders will prefer redwood or cedar because of their resistance to decay. These more expensive woods are very satisfactory but not necessary. For the

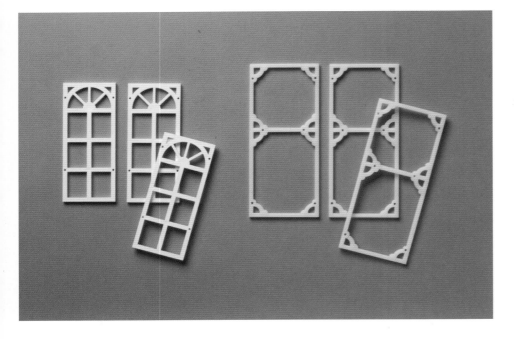

Decorative plastic birdhouse windows and doors are easy to nail on and provide a unique look. (See Appendix - Parts #8606 and #8607.)

Birdhouse Hints

Most birdhouse and birdfeeder projects can be cut with a scroll saw. Access to a table saw will make cutting long straight edges much easier.

projects in this book, you can use inexpensive pine boards. Pine boards are available at all lumberyards and are sold as dimensioned lumber. Dimensioned lumber may consist of various species of pine and other white woods.

For projects that call for plywood, exterior plywood should be used. A very high quality Finnish birch Aircraft grade exterior plywood is available by mail order. A source is listed in the Appendix. Finnish birch plywood has smooth surfaces on both sides and few, if any, interior voids.

PATTERN NOTES

Full-size cutting patterns are provided for pieces that require anything beyond simple cuts (decorative trim, windows, etc.). In a few cases, these patterns are split in half and appear full-size across two separate pages. You are permitted to photocopy these pages within the limits outlined in the copyright notice of this book. These photocopies can be transferred to your wood using

carbon paper or transfer paper. Another method is to glue the photocopied patterns directly to your wood using spray adhesive. These methods are fully described later in this chapter.

Dimensioned drawings are provided for those parts that are too large to put on a page or for those parts that require simple cuts. These drawings have been reduced in size. You can increase them to full size on a photocopier; however, in most cases you can simply transfer the pattern dimensions directly to your wood by making use of layout tools, such as a ruler, a square, a compass and a sharpened No. 2 pencil.

Where holes are required, dimensioned drawings will show the diameter of each hole, the depth it is to be drilled and the location of the hole. The procedure is to use layout tools to measure the location of the center of the holes then mark this center location with a scratch awl. The indentation left by the sharp point of the scratch awl will help prevent the drill bit from wandering when you drill the hole.

As a general rule, dimensioned drawings do not need to be photocopied because you will be using layout tools to transfer the dimensions to the wood.

TRANSFERRING PATTERNS

As mentioned, some of the patterns in this book are drawn full size. You can transfer them directly to your stock using carbon paper or transfer paper. Alternatively, you can make a photocopy of the pattern and glue it directly to your wood. With this method, you will saw through the paper when you cut the wood. Gluing the pattern directly to the wood is the preferred method. It is more accurate than using carbon or transfer paper, and it is also much easier to see the black lines on the white paper. Listed below are some tips for transferring patterns to your wood using three popular methods.

Carbon Paper: Carbon paper has been around for years. It is simply paper with a coating of heavy ink and/or carbon black on one side. To use it, place the ink side on your wood, place the pattern on top and trace the pattern with a pencil. Carbon paper leaves dark lines that are easy to see; however, these lines cannot be erased.

Transfer Paper: Transfer paper is used in the same way as carbon paper. The main difference between carbon and transfer paper is that transfer paper is made from graphite instead of ink or carbon black. With transfer paper, the lines can be erased from your wood using a common pencil eraser.

Glue: Patterns can be glued directly to your wood using spray adhesive. For best results follow this procedure:

1. Make sure the wood is dust free.

2. Spray a light fog of adhesive on the back of the paper pattern. Stop spraying before the paper gets wet, or soaked through with glue. Let the paper dry a few minutes if you have over applied the adhesive.

3. Stick the paper pattern to the wood. Note: Spray adhesive should not be sprayed directly onto the wood itself because this makes both the pattern and the glue residue left on the wood very difficult to remove. With a little experimentation, you will develop a feel for just how much spray adhesive to apply.

Before sawing the piece out, it is a good idea to mark the location of all holes with a scratch awl or center punch. Punch through the pattern and into the wood. But don't drill the holes until after you have finished

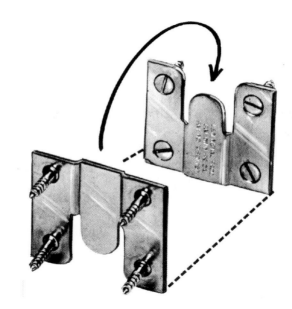

Flush mount hangers are a simple and effective way to hang a birdhouse. One side of the interlocking hanger is attached to the back of the bird-house and the other to a vertical wood post. Lift upward to remove the house for cleaning. (See Appendix - Part #1262.)

cutting out the piece on your scroll saw, otherwise the drill press may rip the paper pattern. Also, by center punching your holes first, you will know where to drill the holes after you have removed the paper pattern.

SELECTING A PROJECT

Begin by paging through the book to decide which projects you wish to make first. Keep in mind the shop equipment you have available. Most projects can be made with a scroll saw and perhaps a drill press or a hand drill. However, for those projects with long straight edges, it will be much easier to cut them if you have access to a table saw.

For each project you will find:

1. a photograph of the finished project,

2. a Bill of Materials listing the size of all wood materials as well as any hardware required,

3. an exploded assembly drawing, or drawings, and

4. individual parts drawings that include full-size drawings for some parts and dimensioned drawings for

Birdhouse Hints

Horizontal saw cuts on the inside of the birdhouse under the entrance hole will help the birds to make their entrance and exit.

Three popular water-based stain-blocking primers. All are recommended for outdoor projects.

Birdhouse Hints

Attach hardware cloth, wood dowels or cleats inside the birdhouse to help young birds gain a good foothold.

other parts.

In a few cases, I have omitted drawing a simple square or rectangular-shaped part. In these instances, the words "not drawn" will appear in parentheses after the listing of that particular part in the Bill of Materials. Simply cut these parts to the widths and lengths given in the Bill of Materials.

BILLS OF MATERIALS

The Bill of Materials lists provide a great deal of useful information. You will find a Bill of Materials for each of the projects within that project's chapter. The first column of the Bill of Materials indicates the number of pieces required. The second column indicates the description or part identification number, if applicable. The last column indicates the size (thickness by width by length) of each piece. When hardware is required, the size—and in some cases a supplier's catalog order number—will be provided. Screws and other fasteners are all readily available and should be easy for you to purchase locally. Other

hardware items, such as plastic birdhouse windows and doors, fiberglass rods, round wood balls and acrylic plastic birdfeeder plates, are more difficult to source. Those items, along with part numbers, are referenced and can be ordered from the supplier listed in the Appendix.

PLANS OF PROCEDURE

As the name implies, the Plan of Procedure tells you how to cut each piece. If a full-size pattern of the piece is provided, the Plan of Procedure step will say "transfer the pattern and cut out." If two or more identical pieces are required, this will be noted (i.e., Two Pieces Required). If a dimensioned drawing is provided, the Plan of Procedure for that piece will say "Lay out and cut to size." For these pieces, transfer the dimensions directly to your wood using layout tools.

FINAL ASSEMBLY INSTRUCTIONS

Once you have cut each individual piece, it will be time to assemble the project and paint it. The Final Assembly Instructions, together with the Assembly Drawings, describe how the pieces of the project fit together. Although the assembly sequence is explained, the choice of fasteners is left, for the most part, to the preferences of the builder. As a general rule, water-resistant glue is recommended, together with either nails or screws.

Remember that birdhouses must be cleaned every year. This is done by removing the top, the bottom or the front. Obviously, whatever piece you choose to remove cannot be glued or nailed during the Final Assembly. Attach this piece with wood screws so it can be removed for cleaning.

In the Tylorville Tudor Apartments Birdhouse and the Adirondack Birdhouse projects, one side is made to pivot on wood dowels or wood screws located near the top of the sidepiece. The bottom of the sidepiece is held in place by one or two wood screws. Remember to make the sidepiece slightly undersized so it won't fit too tight. This recommendation is also true for birdhouses where the floor is inset.

Although not always included on the drawings themselves, ventilation holes should be drilled at the top of every birdhouse. Birdhouses stationed in hotter climates require larger holes than those in cooler climates. Although not shown on the patterns, the top of the left and right sides of some birdhouses can be shortened by ¼" to allow side-to-side ventilation between the sides and the roof.

Drainage holes placed in the floors of all birdhouses are also recommended. Drainage holes can be drilled through a floor using a ¼" to ½" diameter bit. Instead of drilled holes, some projects are pictured with the corners of the floor cut off at 45 degrees.

Natural cavities in tree trunks have irregular surfaces that provide good footholds for birds. This is especially important for young birds so they can get out of the nest. The interiors of the houses in this book are smooth. It will be helpful to the inhabitants if you cut several ⅛" wide by ⅛" deep horizontal saw cuts on the inside of the birdhouse under the entrance hole. Another trick is to attach hardware cloth, wood dowels or other types of cleats to help young birds with their footing.

Do not apply wood finish of any kind to the interior of the house. It will be easier to attract birds if you keep the inside of the nesting cavity as natural as possible.

One of the best ways to support a birdhouse or a birdfeeder is on a post

or a pipe. In this way, you can select the exact height and location. A 4 x 4 cedar, redwood or treated pine post works well. Another good choice is a galvanized steel pipe with a floor flange threaded to the end.

SPECIALTY HARDWARE

In addition to lumber, plywood and paint, some projects require specialty hardware. For those items that may not be easy to locate in most hardware stores, a mail order source is provided in the Appendix at the back of this book.

The Appendix contains a list of all of the specialty hardware that is used and referenced throughout this book. Examples of specialty hardware include plastic birdhouse windows and doors, fiberglass rods, round wood balls and plastic birdfeeder plates.

PAINT AND EFFECTS OF OUTDOOR USE

The harsh effects of outdoor weather are very damaging to wood and paint. It is essential to prepare the surface of any birdhouse or birdfeeder properly and to choose the best primer and paint available. The three most damaging effects to outdoor projects are ultraviolet (UV) radiation, moisture and changes in temperature.

SUNLIGHT AND UV RADIATION

Direct sunshine can degrade the binder and pigment of paint. Binder is the additive in paint that helps it to adhere to the surface being painted. Pigment is the material used to color the paint. Degradation caused by the sun can result in chalking (a white, chalky dust) and loss of color. While all grades of paint suffer these effects to some degree, lower quality paints and interior paints will generally fail much earlier than quality exterior paints.

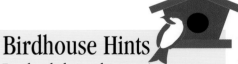

Birdhouse Hints
Perches help predators gain access to a birdhouse more than they help the birds. Most birdhouses do not need them.

Birdhouse Hints

Keep the inside of the nesting cavity as natural as possible. Do not apply wood finish of any kind to the interior of the house.

The binders in acrylic latex paint tend to resist the effects of direct sunlight better than the binders in oil-based paints do. The reason is that the binders used in acrylic latex paints tend to be transparent to UV radiation, while oil binders actually absorb the radiation, which tends to break them down. Red and yellow paint colors are especially vulnerable to fading from UV radiation.

WATER AND MOISTURE

Moisture is especially hard on exterior paint. The source of the moisture can be rain, snow, dew, lawn sprinklers, condensation or humidity from the substrate (the plywood or wood boards). As with UV radiation, moisture tests the paint's resistance to chalking and tint loss. Better grades of acrylic latex paints help to fight these problems better than oil-based paints. This is primarily due to the characteristics of the binders contained in acrylic latex paints.

Water and moisture can also cause

blistering of the paint. When wood gets wet, it expands. When wood dries it contracts. Expansion and contraction of the wood puts great stress on the paint and can result in cracking, flaking and blistering.

Acrylic latex paint is permeable, or breathable, and therefore allows the water to vaporize and escape. High quality acrylic latex paints are very flexible, offering added protection against problems with cracking and flaking.

Never attempt to paint wood that has a high moisture content. Allow wet wood to dry first.

TEMPERATURE CHANGES

Quite naturally, changes in temperature occur to a much greater degree outdoors than they do indoors. Like moisture, temperature changes cause the wood to expand and contract, putting added stress on the paint.

Quality paints that offer both superior adhesion and flexibility help to prevent cracking and flaking. Top quality acrylic latex paint is an especially good choice for exterior applications in areas where there are many heavy freeze/thaw cycles. The acrylic binders that are found in these paints are very durable and offer great flexibility.

CHOOSING THE BEST PRIMER AND PAINT

A primer is defined as a paint coating designed to form a film upon which a succeeding finish coat, or coats, of paint can be applied. Because the outdoor environment places tremendous demands on paint, always purchase the best grade of primer and paint available.

STAIN-BLOCKING PRIMERS

Stain-blocking primers are formulated to prevent stain bleed-through. Stain bleed-through is a brownish or tan discoloration which will appear sometimes several months after the project has been painted. Naturally, it can be quite unsightly, especially on white or light-colored paints. Stain bleed-through can also occur when knots or sap streaks are painted over in any species of wood, including pine lumber and plywood. To avoid stain bleed-through, knots and other lumber defects should be primed with a stain-blocking primer. This will keep the wood tannin from bleeding into the topcoat, except in the most severe cases.

The most common stain-blocking primers are manufactured by Wm. Zinsser & Co., Inc. and Masterchem Industries. Zinsser offers several stain-blocking primers including H2OIL Base, Bulls Eye 1H2H3, Kover-Stain and B-I-N. The most user-friendly products are the H2OIL Base and the Bulls Eye 1H2H3 because soap and water can be used to clean hands and brushes. Masterchem offers KILZ2 and KILZ TOTAL ONE. Both of these products are satisfactory for spot priming knots and other lumber defects, and both feature soap and water cleanup.

APPLICATION

After spot priming the knots, one coat of primer should be applied prior to painting any subsequent coats. Paint should not be used in place of primer. The reason is that primer contains less pigment, which allows it to better soak into the wood for a more adhesive grip.

Birdhouse Hints
Red and yellow paint colors are especially vulnerable to fading from Ultraviolet radiation.

	Latex	Oil
Drying Time	1-4 hours	24-48 hours
Vehicle	Non-flammable Minimal offensive odor	Flammable Toxic, mineral based
Fumes	Minimal risk of inhalation	Toxic. If used indoors, must be well-ventilated
Liquid Used for Thinning	Water	Paint thinner or turpentine
Cleanup	Warm water and soap	Paint thinner or, turpentine; must be well-ventilated

Don't apply extra-heavy coats of either primer or paint. An extra-heavy coat will not necessarily offer better protection. In fact, coats that are too thick will probably crack, which will result in less protection.

Always follow the label instructions. Manufacturers put a great deal of effort into the research and development of their paint products. It is a good idea to get in the habit of reading and following label instructions.

LATEX VERSUS OIL

Acrylic latex primers and gloss or semi-gloss acrylic latex exterior paints are recommended for outdoor wood projects. This is not to say that oil-based primers and paints cannot be used. Oil-based primers do have their advantages. For example, they are better suited to hide imperfections and therefore have better coverage. They also offer better adhesion to wood and therefore seal the surface better. However, after considerable experimenting, I have found acrylic latex primer and paint to be the all-around best choice for painting outdoor projects. The chart on page 7 outlines some of the advantages of latex versus oil primers and paints.

SELECTING THE PAINT FOR THE TOP COATS

Select the best quality of paint available to top coat your projects. Paint for the top coats should also be compatible with the primer you have chosen. Look for exterior trim paint or trim and shutter paint. Trim paints are formulated for exterior wood trim areas of homes. They are available in gloss or semi-gloss finishes, both of which are recommended finishes for birdhouses and birdfeeders.

When you purchase paints, be sure to have your dealer shake them. This will ensure that all of the pigment is suspended evenly throughout the paint. Also, be sure to ask the paint dealer for complimentary wooden stir sticks. Use these wood sticks to mix the paint immediately upon opening the can, and periodically when you are painting, to be absolutely sure that the color and pigment stay evenly distributed. Many hobbyists consider the painting of the final coat to be the most enjoyable part of making the project.

The choice of paint colors is entirely up to the builder. If you have house paint left over and you want your birdhouse or birdfeeder to match your house, by all means use it. I have specified paint colors on the individual drawings of each piece. If you like the way the project looks in the color photograph, simply paint the pieces as specified.

FULL SIZE DRAWINGS

Large plan sheets that include full-size patterns are available for each of the birdhouses and birdfeeders in this book. These plan sheets can be purchased from the author. See the ordering information following the appendix.

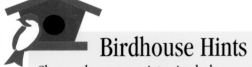

Birdhouse Hints
Choose the appropriate size hole for the birds that will inhabit your birdhouse.

Part Two
Birdhouses

Adirondack Birdhouse

In the early 1900s, the Adirondack Mountains of New York were beginning to become a popular tourist destination. It was in these tourist resorts that the popular Adirondack chair originated. These chairs varied in appearance among builders, but many shared the same general styling.

I have had the pleasure of designing my own version of this chair, after which I designed a matching loveseat. Then came a glider. Next I made a coffee table and an end table, then a picnic bench and finally a wishing well. All of these projects, as well as this birdhouse, share the same Adirondack styling elements and design features.

You'll find this birdhouse to be an easy project that uses all ¾" stock. After you've finished it, your next project can be the Adirondack chair, then the loveseat, etc.

PLAN OF PROCEDURE

This project is constructed primarily from ¾" stock. I used one eight-foot piece of 1x10 pine.

The entrance hole can be cut in the tree shape, as shown, or in a more traditional circular shape.

The Back piece extends below the Floor of the house. Drill screw clearance holes. Drive screws through these holes when mounting the project to a post or a tree trunk.

Back: Lay out and cut to size from ¾" stock.

Front: Lay out and cut to size from ¾" stock.

Roof #1 and #2: Lay out and cut to size from ¾" stock.

Side: Lay out and cut to size from ¾" stock. Cut the 45-degree bevel. (Two Pieces Required)

Floor: Lay out and cut to size from ¾" stock. Cut the 45-degree notches for drainage.

FINAL ASSEMBLY:

Paint: Acrylic latex primer and gloss or semi-gloss exterior acrylic latex paint are recommended. I used white primer, winter white and forest green for this project.

Step 1: Attach one Side and the Floor to the Back where shown. Attach the Front to the Side and Floor. Attach Roof #1 and Roof #2 to the Side, Front and Back.

Step 2: The remaining Side is made to swing open for cleaning and should not be glued in place. Fit this remaining Side piece so that it slips in place between the Front and the Back.

Step 3: Drive two nails through the Front and the Back and into the Side. The Side should fit loose enough so that it will swing open for cleaning. Secure the bottom of the Side to the Floor with a screw. To clean, remove the retaining screw and swing open the Side.

Step 4: Paint the project as desired.

Step 5: Mount the finished project to a tree or a post.

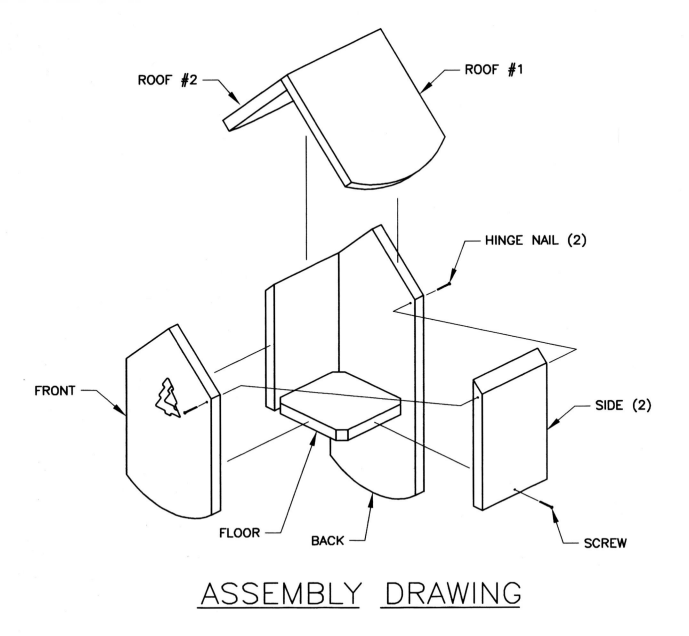

ROOF #2

ROOF #1

HINGE NAIL (2)

FRONT

SIDE (2)

FLOOR

BACK

SCREW

ASSEMBLY DRAWING

ADIRONDACK BIRDHOUSE: BILL OF MATERIALS

Quantity	Description	Size of Material
1	Back	¾" x 7¼" x 19"
1	Front	¾" x 7¼" x 13¼"
1	Roof #1	¾" x 8" x 9"
1	Roof #2	¾" x 8" x 8¼"
2	Side	¾" x 5½" x 9⅛"
1	Floor	¾" x 5½" x 5¾"

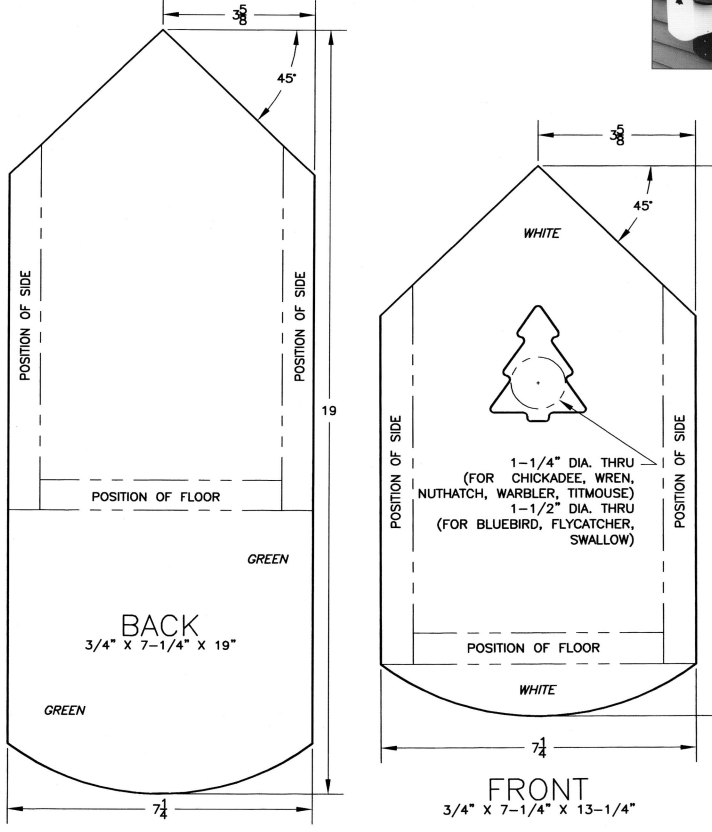

BACK
3/4" X 7-1/4" X 19"

POSITION OF SIDE

POSITION OF SIDE

POSITION OF FLOOR

GREEN

GREEN

5/8

45°

19

7 1/4

FRONT
3/4" X 7-1/4" X 13-1/4"

WHITE

POSITION OF SIDE

POSITION OF SIDE

1-1/4" DIA. THRU
(FOR CHICKADEE, WREN,
NUTHATCH, WARBLER, TITMOUSE)
1-1/2" DIA. THRU
(FOR BLUEBIRD, FLYCATCHER,
SWALLOW)

POSITION OF FLOOR

WHITE

5/8

45°

7 1/4

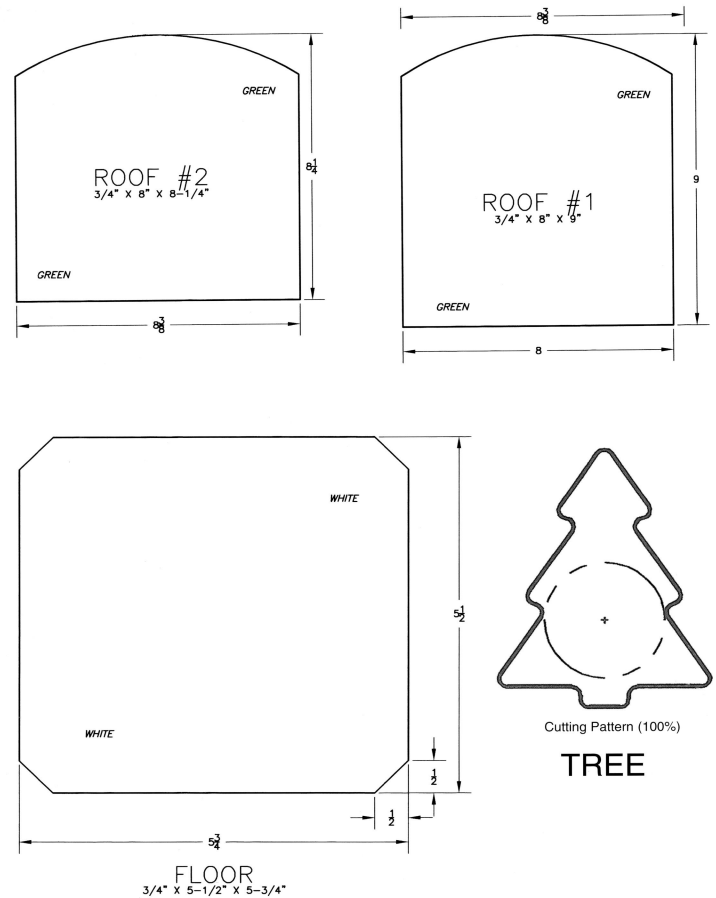

ROOF #2
3/4" x 8" x 8-1/4"

GREEN

GREEN

$8\frac{1}{4}$

$8\frac{3}{8}$

ROOF #1
3/4" x 8" x 9"

GREEN

GREEN

$8\frac{3}{8}$

9

8

WHITE

WHITE

$5\frac{1}{2}$

$5\frac{3}{4}$

$\frac{1}{2}$

$\frac{1}{2}$

FLOOR
3/4" x 5-1/2" x 5-3/4"

Cutting Pattern (100%)

TREE

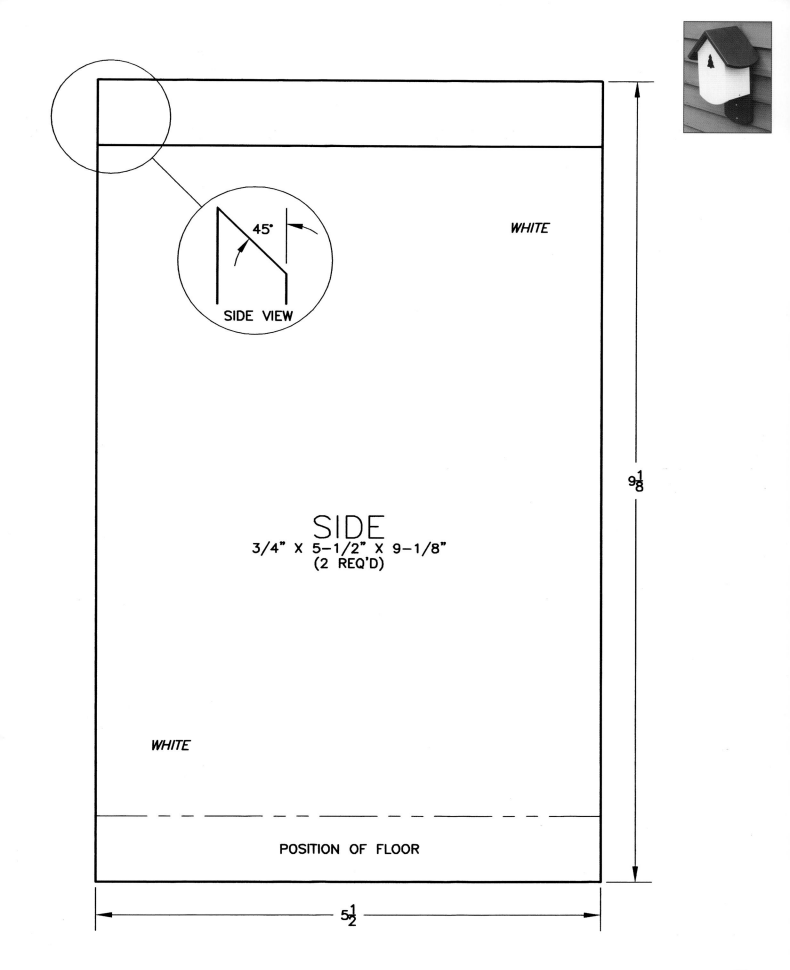

45°

SIDE VIEW

WHITE

SIDE
3/4" X 5–1/2" X 9–1/8"
(2 REQ'D)

$9\frac{1}{8}$

WHITE

POSITION OF FLOOR

$5\frac{1}{2}$

Adobe Birdhouse

The dictionary definition of the word adobe is "unburnt, sun-dried brick;" also, "a structure built of such material as seen in the southwest United States and Mexico."

So the question becomes, how does one make a plywood birdhouse look like real adobe? I felt the answer was to incorporate some of the classic styling features such as the ladder, the drying posts and the cacti. All of these characteristics help to accent the general architectural shape.

The final touch is the builder's choice of paint colors. I chose a dull pink for the building and a kelly green for the plants.

PLAN OF PROCEDURE

Layout and cut all pieces to size according to the dimensions given in the Bill of Materials. Drill all holes as required. Finish-sand all parts. The assembly steps refer to the step-by-step illustrations on page 19. The Roof pieces are attached with screws so they can be removed to clean the birdhouse. The Door is glued to the Front for appearance purposes only.

Step 1: Nail and glue the Back, Front and Side pieces together as shown.

Step 2: Attach the Roof pieces to the Sides and Backs with the 1¼" Wood Screws.

Step 3: Glue the Door and Ladder to the Front pieces. Glue the ¾" diameter Dowels in the ⅜" holes in the Front pieces.

FINAL ASSEMBLY

Glue the completed house assembly to the Ground piece in the position shown. Glue the Cacti to the Front pieces. Paint as desired. (You may wish to paint some parts prior to assembly.)

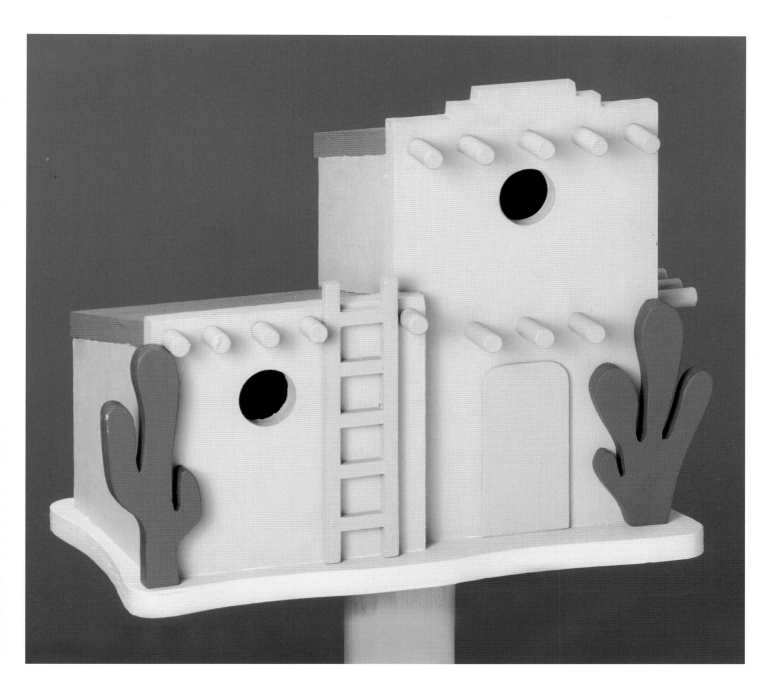

Birdhouse Hints

Remove old nests from birdhouses and nesting shelves to lessen the chance of parasite infestations.

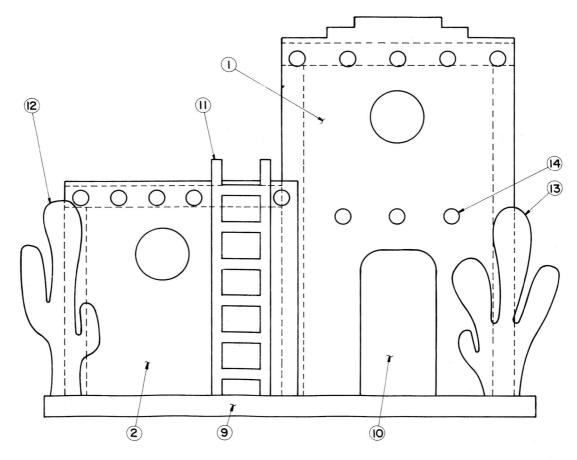

ADOBE BIRDHOUSE: BILL OF MATERIALS

Quantity	Part #	Description	Size of Material
1	#1	Front	½" x 5⅜" x 9"
1	#2	Front	½" x 5⅜" x 5⅛"
2	#3	Sides	½" x 4½" x 7⅞"
1	#4	Side	½" x 4½" x 5"
1	#5	Back	½" x 4⅜" x 6¹¹⁄₁₆"
1	#6	Back	½" x 3³⁄₁₆" x 4½"
1	#7	Roof	½" x 5" x 5⅜"
1	#8	Roof	½" x 5" x 5½"
1	#9	Ground	½" x 6⅝" x 11⅜"
1	#10	Door	¼" x 1¾" x 3½"
1	#11	Ladder	¼" x 1⅜" x 5⅝"
1	#12	Cactus	½" x 1⅞" x 4¾"
1	#13	Cactus	½" x 2½" x 4 ½"
13	#14	Dowels	⅜" dia x 1⅜"
8	#15	*Wood Screws	1¼" x #8

*Available from Meisel Hardware Specialties.

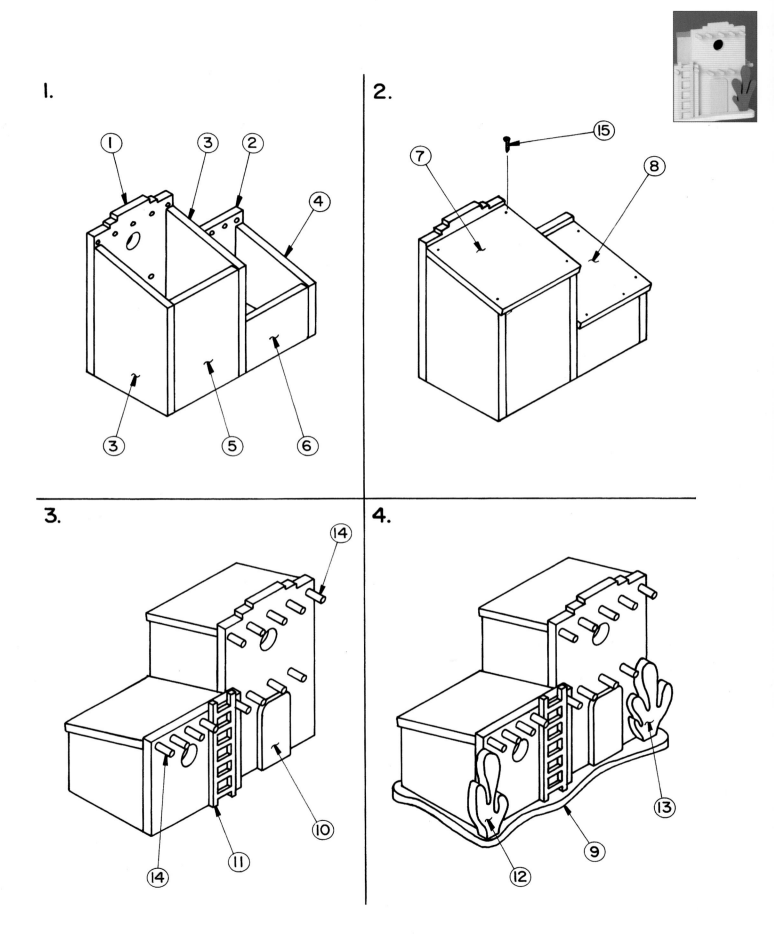

1.

2.

3.

4.

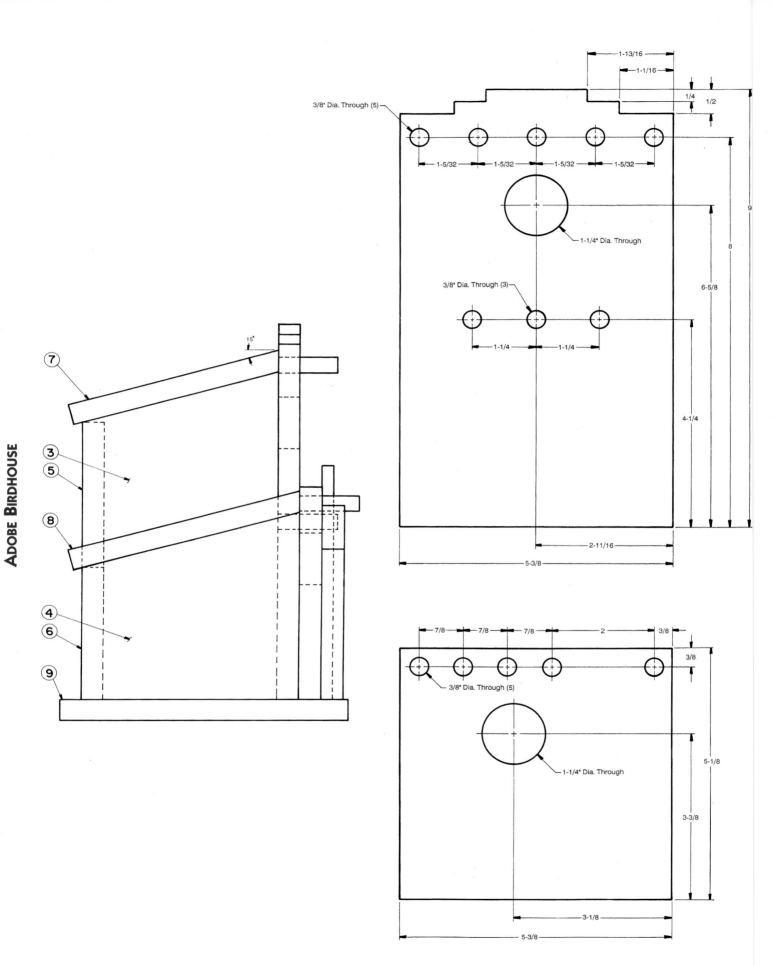

3/8" Dia. Through (5)

1-13/16
1-1/16
1/4
1/2

1-5/32 · 1-5/32 · 1-5/32 · 1-5/32

1-1/4" Dia. Through

3/8" Dia. Through (3)

1-1/4 · 1-1/4

9
8
6-5/8
4-1/4

2-11/16
5-3/8

7/8 · 7/8 · 7/8 · 2 · 3/8

3/8

3/8" Dia. Through (5)

1-1/4" Dia. Through

5-1/8
3-3/8

3-1/8
5-3/8

15°

7
3
5
8
4
6
9

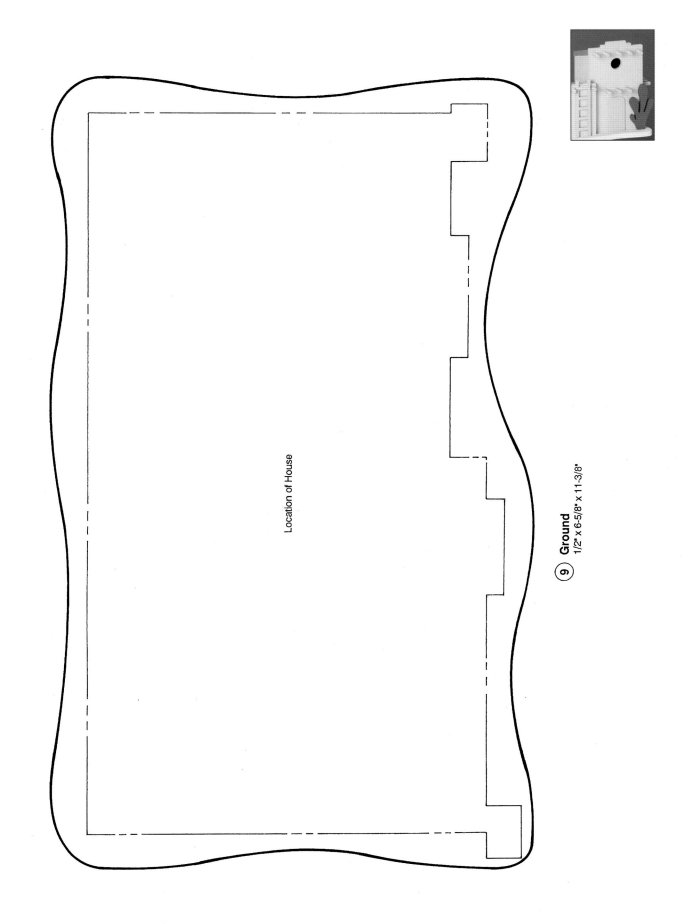

Location of House

Ⓞ Ground
1/2" x 6-5/8" x 11-3/8"

American Home Birdhouse

This birdhouse has two components that can be seen on many homes, especially older homes: the add-on porch and the bay window.

Because porches are often added to the home some years after the house is first built, it is natural that many have an added-on appearance. Although you'll actually be building this house and the porch at the same time, I wanted the design to reflect that added-on look.

The bay window is another fun feature. I've never seen it used on a birdhouse before. It is made from a short length of 2x6 stock. A table saw is used to cut the bevels on each side. A compound miter box saw can be used to cut the detail on top (or you can cut them with a handsaw). You'll wind up with a piece shaped like a bay window. Sure it's a fairly heavy piece to attach to the front of the house, but so what? It's the bay window look that you want to achieve. Nail on the plastic windows (after you have finished painting the house).

Because these design elements are so common in American homes, I call this project the American Home Birdhouse.

PLAN OF PROCEDURE

The main structure of the house itself is cut from ¾" lumber. A short length of 2x6 stock can be used to cut the chimney and bay window.

The Front and Back piece are identical in size. The only difference is that the entrance hole is drilled on the front piece only. The window and door are mounted on the Front piece.

Front/Back: Lay out and cut to size from ¾" stock. Drill the 1¼"-diameter hole through the Front piece only. (One Front and one Back piece required)

Roof #1: Lay out and cut to size from ¾" stock. Cut the 45-degree bevel.

Roof #2: Lay out and cut to size from ¾" stock. Cut the 45-degree bevel. (Two Pieces Required)

Bay Window: Lay out and cut to size from 1½" stock. Cut the 35- and 45-degree bevels as shown in the Top, Front and Right Side View Drawings.

Left Side #1 and Left Side #2: Lay out and cut to size from ¾" stock. Cut the 45-degree bevel.

Floor: Lay out and cut to size from ¾" stock. Cut the corner notches as shown.

Right Side: Lay out and cut to size from ¾" stock. Cut the 45-degree bevel.

Step & Chimney Top: Lay out and cut to size from ¾" stock.

Cornice: Transfer pattern onto ¼" stock and cut out.

Brace: Transfer pattern onto ¾" stock and cut out. (Two Pieces Required)

Chimney: Lay out and cut to size from 1½" stock. Cut the 45-degree bevel

FINAL ASSEMBLY

Step 1: Attach the Front and Back pieces to the Side pieces.

Step 2: Attach the Floor using wood screws through the Sides and Back pieces so that the Floor can be removed for cleaning.

Step 3: Attach the Roof pieces so the back edge is flush with the Back piece. The Roof pieces should overlap the Front piece by ½". Attach the Cornice as shown.

Step 4: Attach the Braces and the Bay Window. The bottom of the Braces should be flush with the bottom of the Front piece. Install the Step as shown on the drawing of the Front/Back piece.

Step 5: Install the Chimney Top centered on top of the Chimney piece. Attach the Chimney to the left side of the Roof #2 piece. The Chimney should be centered between the front and back with the top of the Chimney assembly the same height as the Roof peak.

Paint: Paint the project before attaching the windows and doors. Acrylic latex primer and gloss or semi-gloss exterior acrylic latex paint are recommended. I used winter white for this project.

Step 6: Attach the Birdhouse Windows and Birdhouse Door with the Escutcheon Pins.

AMERICAN HOME BIRDHOUSE BILL OF MATERIALS

Quantity	Description	Size of Material
2	Front/Back	¾" x 7¾" x 13"
1	Roof #1	¾" x 4¾" x 6"
2	Roof #2	¾" x 5½" x 6"
1	Bay Window	1½" x 5¼" x 5¼"
1	Left Side #1	¾" x 4" x 6¼"
1	Left Side #2	¾" x 3¼" x 4"
1	Floor	¾" x 4" x 6¼"
1	Right Side	¾" x 4" x 11"
1	Step	¾" x 1½" x 2¼"
1	Cornice	¼" x 1" x 1"
2	Brace	¾" x 1¼" x 1½"
1	Chimney	1½" x 1½" x 2"
1	Chimney Top	¾" x 2" x 2"
7	*Birdhouse Window (#8607)	1½" x 3½"
1	*Birdhouse Door (#8606)	2" x 4½"
34	*Escutcheon Pin (#388)	⅜" x #18

*Available from Meisel Hardware Specialties.

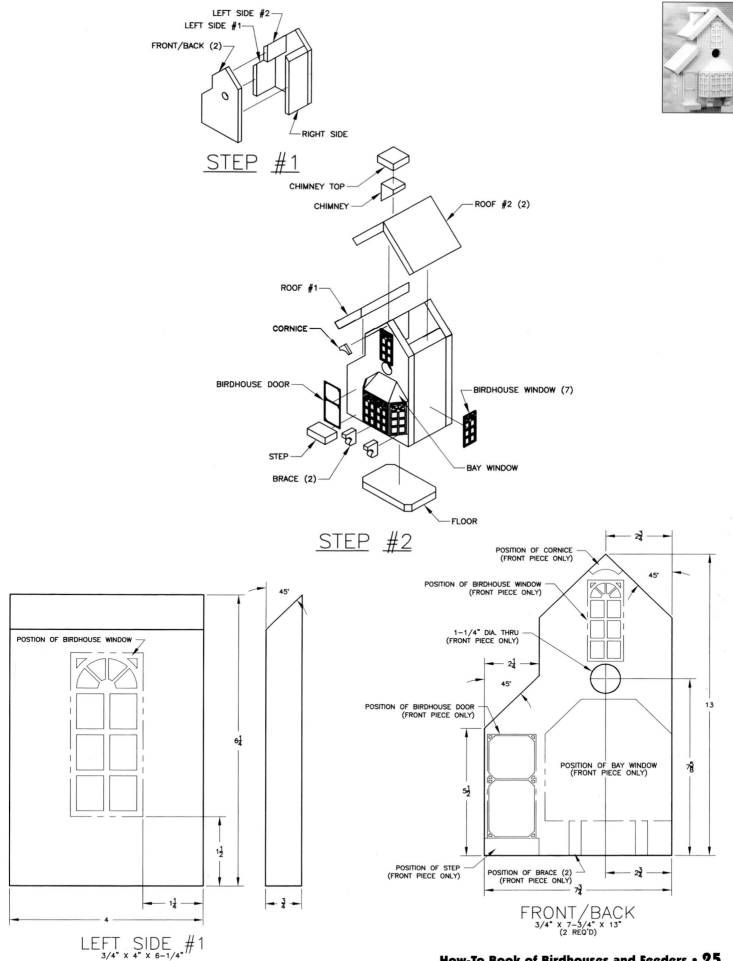

LEFT SIDE #2
LEFT SIDE #1
FRONT/BACK (2)

RIGHT SIDE

STEP #1

CHIMNEY TOP

CHIMNEY

ROOF #2 (2)

ROOF #1

CORNICE

BIRDHOUSE DOOR

BIRDHOUSE WINDOW (7)

STEP

BRACE (2)

BAY WINDOW

FLOOR

STEP #2

POSTION OF BIRDHOUSE WINDOW

45°

$6\frac{1}{4}$

$1\frac{1}{2}$

$1\frac{1}{4}$

$\frac{3}{4}$

4

LEFT SIDE #1
3/4" X 4" X 6-1/4"

POSITION OF CORNICE
(FRONT PIECE ONLY)

POSITION OF BIRDHOUSE WINDOW
(FRONT PIECE ONLY)

1-1/4" DIA. THRU
(FRONT PIECE ONLY)

POSITION OF BIRDHOUSE DOOR
(FRONT PIECE ONLY)

POSITION OF BAY WINDOW
(FRONT PIECE ONLY)

POSITION OF STEP
(FRONT PIECE ONLY)

POSITION OF BRACE (2)
(FRONT PIECE ONLY)

$2\frac{3}{4}$

45°

$2\frac{1}{4}$

45°

$5\frac{1}{2}$

13

$7\frac{5}{8}$

$2\frac{3}{4}$

$7\frac{3}{4}$

FRONT/BACK
3/4" X 7-3/4" X 13"
(2 REQ'D)

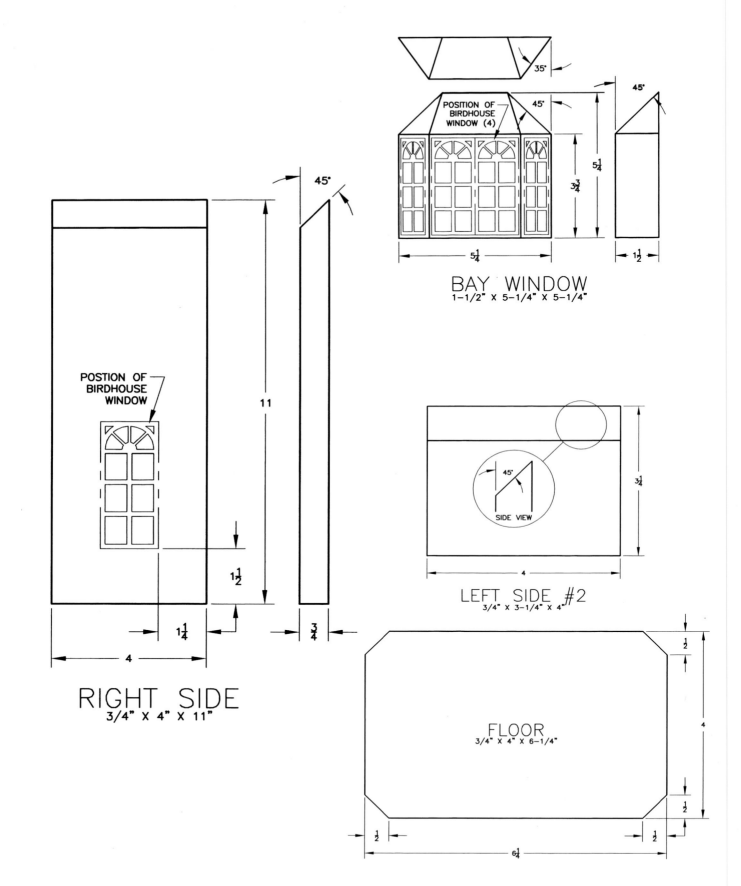

35°

POSITION OF
BIRDHOUSE
WINDOW (4)

45°

45°

5¼

3¾

1½

BAY WINDOW
1-1/2" X 5-1/4" X 5-1/4"

5¼

45°

11

POSTION OF
BIRDHOUSE
WINDOW

45°
SIDE VIEW

3¼

4

LEFT SIDE #2
3/4" X 3-1/4" X 4"

1½

1¼

4

¾

RIGHT SIDE
3/4" X 4" X 11"

½

½

4

½

FLOOR
3/4" X 4" X 6-1/4"

½

6¼

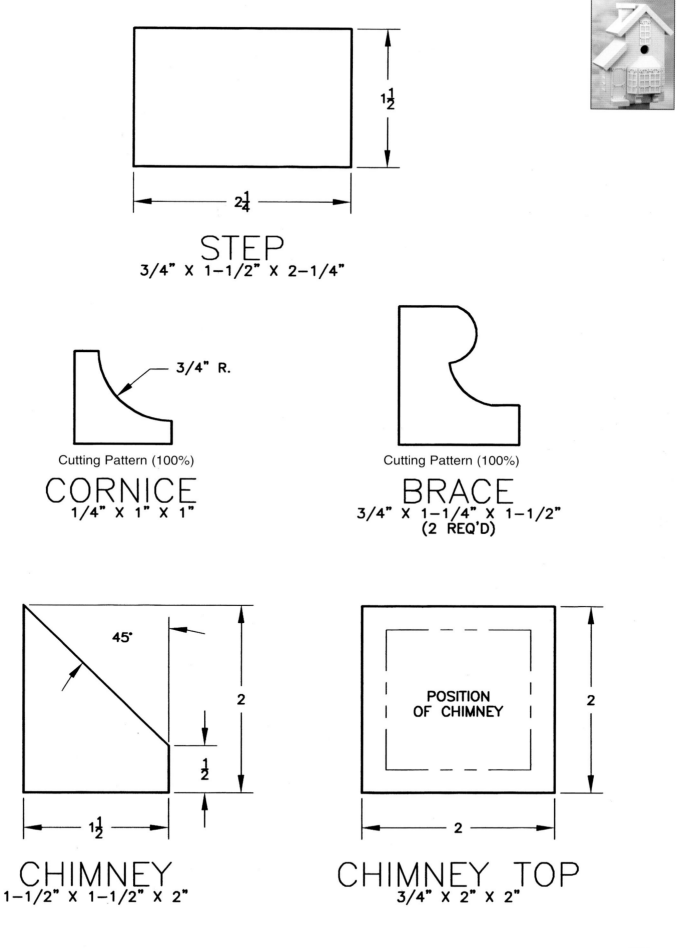

STEP
3/4" X 1-1/2" X 2-1/4"

Cutting Pattern (100%)

3/4" R.

CORNICE
1/4" X 1" X 1"

Cutting Pattern (100%)

BRACE
3/4" X 1-1/4" X 1-1/2"
(2 REQ'D)

45°

CHIMNEY
1-1/2" X 1-1/2" X 2"

POSITION
OF CHIMNEY

CHIMNEY TOP
3/4" X 2" X 2"

Basement Birdhouse

I grew up in the Minneapolis area. Every house had a basement. I loved the basement. I got my start in woodworking in my Dad's workshop down in our basement. I know that in warmer climates, many people set up their workshops in their garage; but in Minnesota, the basement is the common choice for a workshop location.

Money was tight back in the 1950s and 1960s. To save money, people would sometimes build only the basement and then cap it off with a flat roof covered with tarpaper. An entryway was built with a door that led immediately to the stairway. They called these "basement homes."

My mother had a cousin who lived in one. Every time we went to visit, my mother would remind me never to say anything about the condition of her home. The main thing I remember was that the tarpapered, flat roof leaked. I always felt that we were visiting the poor side of our extended family.

I suppose that very few people remember basement houses; however, I guess it would be fair to say that I designed this Basement Birdhouse for those people who might be old enough to remember what a basement house even is!

PLAN OF PROCEDURE

The step-by-step drawings, as well as the Front and Side view drawings, show how all of the pieces are assembled. The rectangular shaped pieces are cut to the length and width given in the Bill of Materials. The Entrance piece (#5) is cut diagonally from a 1½" piece of stock. I used a scrap of 2x4. The Entrance Roof piece is cut from ¼" exterior plywood with a 45-degree angle at the bottom.

Construction is primarily from ½" exterior plywood. Begin by cutting the Front, Back, Floor, Sides and Roof pieces to the dimensions given in the Bill of Materials.

The Ground piece is cut with an irregular shape to suggest the lawn or surface of the earth. It contains a ¼"-diameter hole for the Mailbox Post and ½"-diameter holes for the Fence Posts. The Door and Flag are cut from ⅛" exterior plywood. The Mailbox Post, Fence Post and Fence Rails are cut from Wood Dowels. A brass Escutcheon Pin is used as a door knob.

Step 1: Glue and nail the Back, Sides and Front. Attach the Front to the Sides with wood screws so you will be able to remove the Front piece to clean the birdhouse.

Step 2: Glue and nail the Ground piece to the Sides and Back. Do not glue the Front piece. Glue the Roof piece to the Ground. Glue the Entrance piece to the Roof. Glue the Door and Entrance Roof to the Entrance piece.

Step 3: Glue the Mailbox Post in the ¼" hole in the Ground. Glue the Mailbox to the Mailbox Post and the Flag to the Mailbox. Assemble the Fence Posts and Fence Rails and glue the Fence Posts in the ½" holes in the Ground piece.

Step 4: Glue the Tree and Tree Sides together and glue them to the Ground piece.

FINAL ASSEMBLY

Galvanized or PVC pipe and a floor flange is the best mounting method, although a wood post can also be used. You may wish to drill ¼" ventilation holes in the upper part of the front and back of the birdhouse, just underneath the overhang of the Ground. Also, drill two ¼" drainage holes through the Floor of the birdhouse.

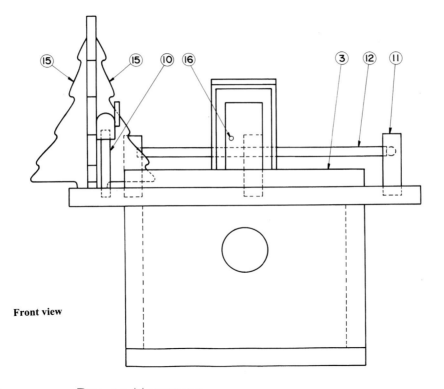

Front view

BASEMENT BIRDHOUSE: BILL OF MATERIALS

Quantity	Part #	Description	Size of Material
2	1	Front & Back	½" x 4" x 6½"
2	2	Sides	½" x 4" x 5½"
2	3	Floor & Roof	½" x 6½" x 6½"
1	4	Ground	½" x 9" x 9½"
1	5	Entrance	1½" x 2¼" x 2¼"
1	6	Entrance Roof	¼" x 1¾" x 3⅝"
1	7	Door	⅛" x 1" x 1⅞"
1	8	Mailbox	½" x ¾" x 1¼"
1	9	Flag	⅛" x ¼" x ¾"
1	10	Mailbox Post	¼" Dia. x 1⅞"
5	11	Fence Post	½" Dia. x 1¾"
1	12	Fence Rail	¼" Dia. x 6¾"
1	13	Fence Rail	¼" Dia. x 7½"
1	14	Tree	¼" x 3⅜" x 4¾"
2	15	Tree Sides	¼" x 1⅝" x 4¼"
1	16	*Escutcheon Pin	⅜" x #18 (#388)
4	17	*Wood Screws	1¼" x #8 (WS1148)

*Available from Meisel Hardware Specialties.

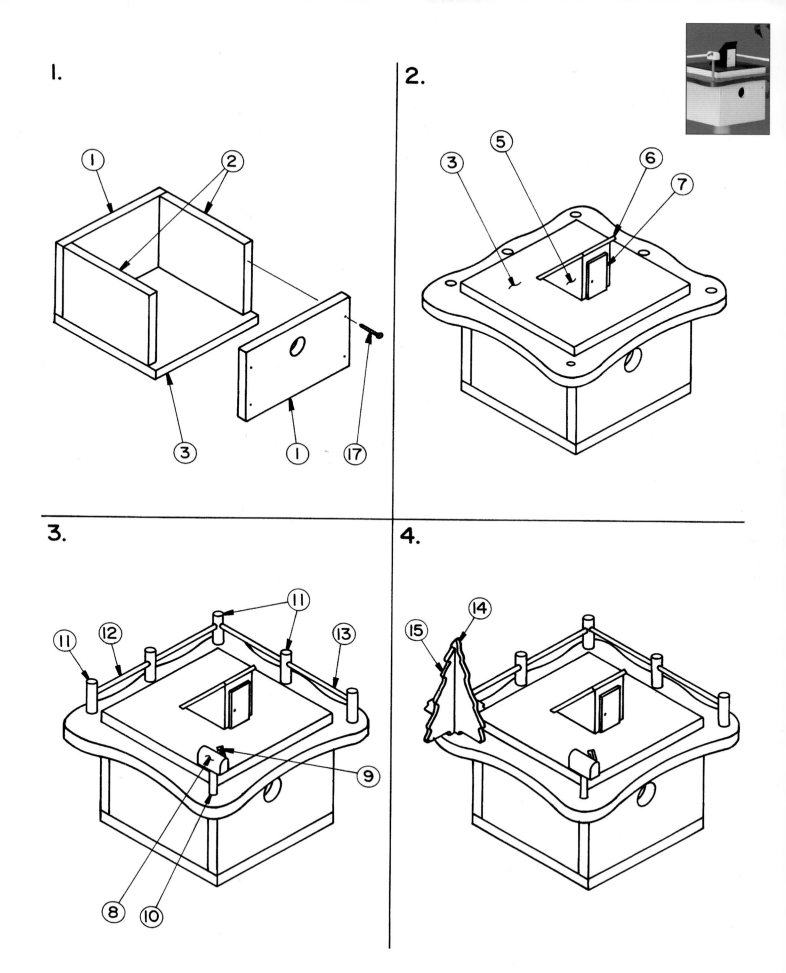

1.

2.

3.

4.

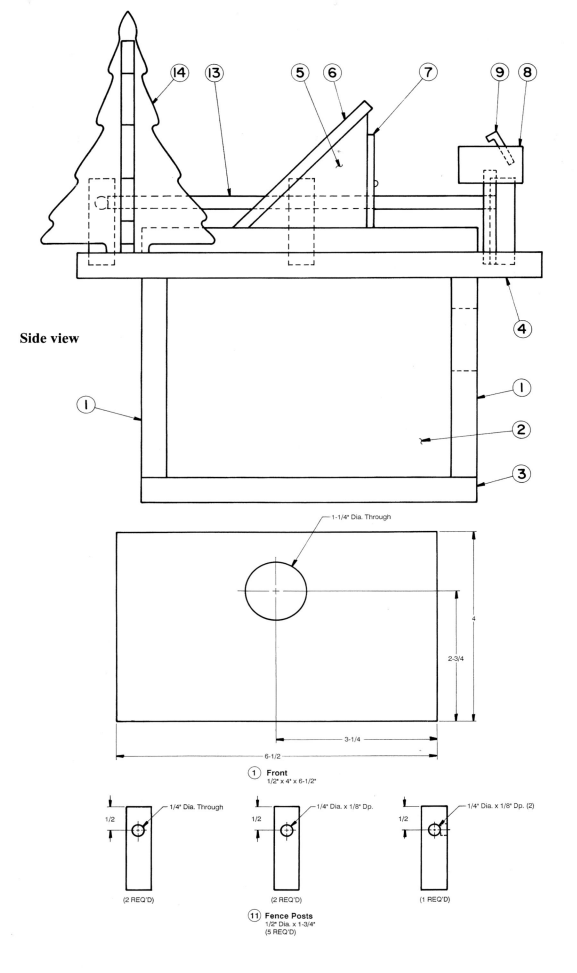

Side view

1-1/4" Dia. Through

4

2-3/4

3-1/4

6-1/2

1 **Front**
1/2" x 4" x 6-1/2"

1/4" Dia. Through

1/2

(2 REQ'D)

1/4" Dia. x 1/8" Dp.

1/2

(2 REQ'D)

1/4" Dia. x 1/8" Dp. (2)

1/2

(1 REQ'D)

11 **Fence Posts**
1/2" Dia. x 1-3/4"
(5 REQ'D)

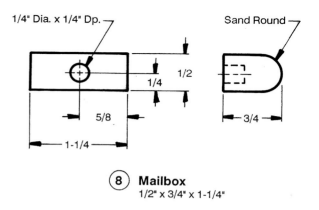

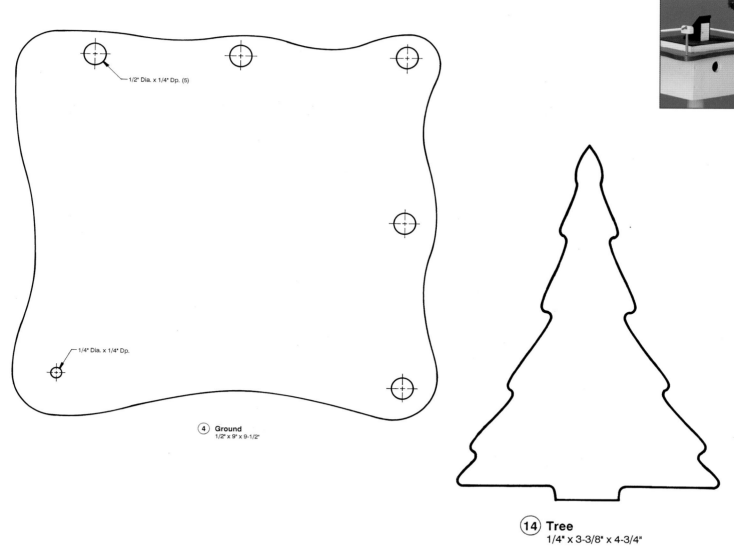

1/2" Dia. x 1/4" Dp. (5)

1/4" Dia. x 1/4" Dp.

(4) **Ground**
1/2" x 9" x 9-1/2"

(14) **Tree**
1/4" x 3-3/8" x 4-3/4"

1/4" Dia. x 1/4" Dp.

Sand Round

1/2

1/4

5/8

1-1/4

3/4

(8) **Mailbox**
1/2" x 3/4" x 1-1/4"

Country Church Birdhouse

This is a very simple design that uses plastic birdhouse windows and plastic columns for accents. I call it the Country Church because it reminds me of the small country churches so common throughout my home state of Minnesota.

Although the birdhouse windows are readily available from the source mentioned in the Appendix of this book, the plastic columns are not. The columns I used are manufactured by Wilton and are sold in stores that specialize in wedding cakes. Anyone in your town who makes wedding cakes should be able to get them for you. They come in several sizes. Be sure to get the ones that are 7" high for this project.

PLAN OF PROCEDURE

Most parts are cut from a 1x8 piece of pine. A length of 2x2 was used for the steeple.

If you can't find plastic columns, you can make your own using 7/8" wood dowels with a 1 3/16" x 1 3/16" square of 1/4" plywood on each end.

The two crosses on the steeple can be cut from 1/4" exterior plywood. Paint them with gold acrylic latex primer and gloss or semi-gloss exterior acrylic latex paint.

Pillar Support: Lay out and cut to size from 3/4" stock. (Two Pieces Required)

Floor: Lay out and cut to size from 3/4" stock. Cut the corners as shown.

Front/Back: Lay out and cut to size from 3/4" stock. Drill the 2 1/8"-diameter hole through the Front piece only. (One Front and One Back Piece Required)

Roof: Lay out and cut to size from 3/4" stock. Cut the 45-degree bevel. (Two Pieces Required)

Side: Lay out and cut to size from 3/4" stock. Cut the 45-degree bevel. (Two Pieces Required)

Front Trim: Lay out and cut to size from 3/4" stock. Drill the 1 1/4"-diameter hole.

Steeple: Lay out and cut to size from 1 1/2" stock. Cut the 20-degree bevels on all four sides to make the point at the top. Cut the 45-degree notch in the bottom so it will fit on the Roof.

Cross: Transfer the Cross pattern from the Steeple to 1/4" stock and cut to size. (Two Pieces Required)

FINAL ASSEMBLY:

Step 1: Attach the Front and the Back pieces to the Side pieces. Attach the Floor with wood screws through the Sides and Back pieces, but not the Front piece, so that the Floor can be removed for cleaning.

Step 2: Attach the Roof pieces flush with the Back piece. The Roof pieces should overlap the Front piece by 1/2". Attach the Pillar Support and the Front Trim piece to the Front where shown. Temporarily position the Plastic Pillars to be sure the spacing of the Pillar Supports is correct. Do not install the Plastic Pillars until after the project has been painted.

Step 3: Attach the Steeple to the top of the Roof (1/2" from the front edge). Glue the Crosses to the front and back of the Steeple.

Paint: Paint the project as desired. Acrylic latex primer and gloss or semi-gloss exterior acrylic latex paint are recommended. I used winter white, white primer and forest green for this project.

Attach the Birdhouse Windows with the Escutcheon Pins. Glue the Plastic Pillars in place with silicone glue.

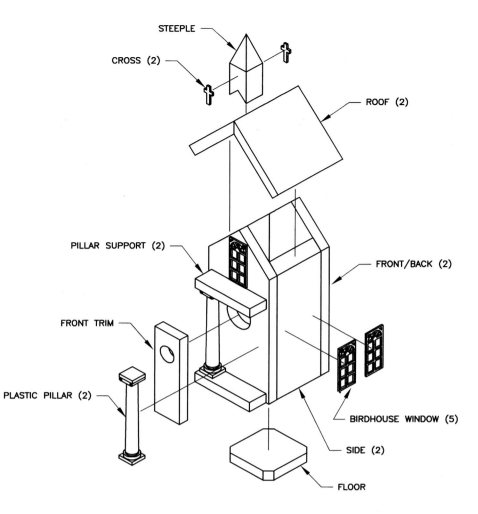

STEEPLE

CROSS (2)

ROOF (2)

PILLAR SUPPORT (2)

FRONT/BACK (2)

FRONT TRIM

PLASTIC PILLAR (2)

BIRDHOUSE WINDOW (5)

SIDE (2)

FLOOR

ASSEMBLY DRAWING

COUNTRY CHURCH BIRDHOUSE: BILL OF MATERIALS

Quantity	Description	Size of Material
2	Pillar Support	¾" x 1½" x 5"
1	Floor	¾" x 4" x 4"
2	Front/Back	¾" x 5½" x 13"
2	Roof	¾" x 5¾" x 5⅞"
2	Side	¾" x 4" x 11"
1	Front Trim	¾" x 2¼" x 7"
1	Steeple	1½" x 1½" x 4⅝"
2	Cross	¼" x ¾" x 1 ½"
2	Plastic Pillar	1³⁄₁₆" x 7"
5	*Birdhouse Window (#8607)	1½" x 3½"
20	*Escutcheon Pin (#388)	⅜" x #18

*Available from Meisel Hardware Specialties.

PILLAR SUPPORT
3/4" x 1-1/2" x 5"
(2 REQ'D)

$1\frac{1}{2}$

5

FLOOR
3/4" x 4" x 4"

4

4

$\frac{1}{2}$

$\frac{1}{2}$

$\frac{1}{2}$

$\frac{1}{2}$

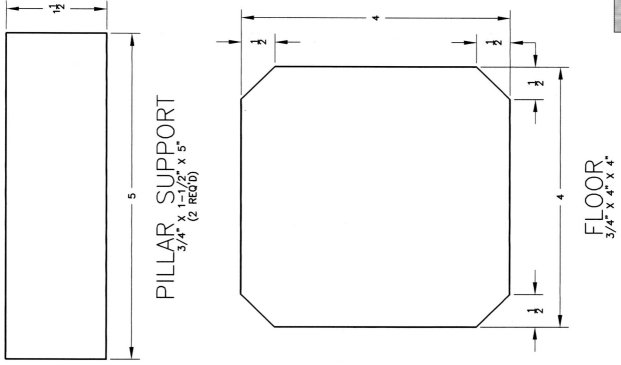

FRONT/BACK
3/4" x 5-1/2" x 13"
(2 REQ'D)

13

$10\frac{1}{4}$

6

45°

POSITION OF WINDOW
(FRONT PIECE ONLY)

POSITION OF PILLAR SUPPORT
(FRONT PIECE ONLY)

POSITION OF SIDE
(OTHER SIDE)

POSITION OF FRONT TRIM
(FRONT PIECE ONLY)

POSITION OF SIDE
(OTHER SIDE)

POSITION OF PILLAR SUPPORT
(FRONT PIECE ONLY)

2-1/8" DIA. THRU
(FRONT PIECE ONLY)

$2\frac{3}{4}$

$5\frac{1}{2}$

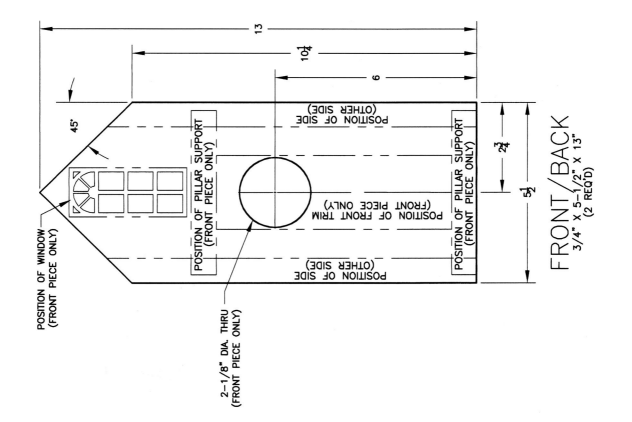

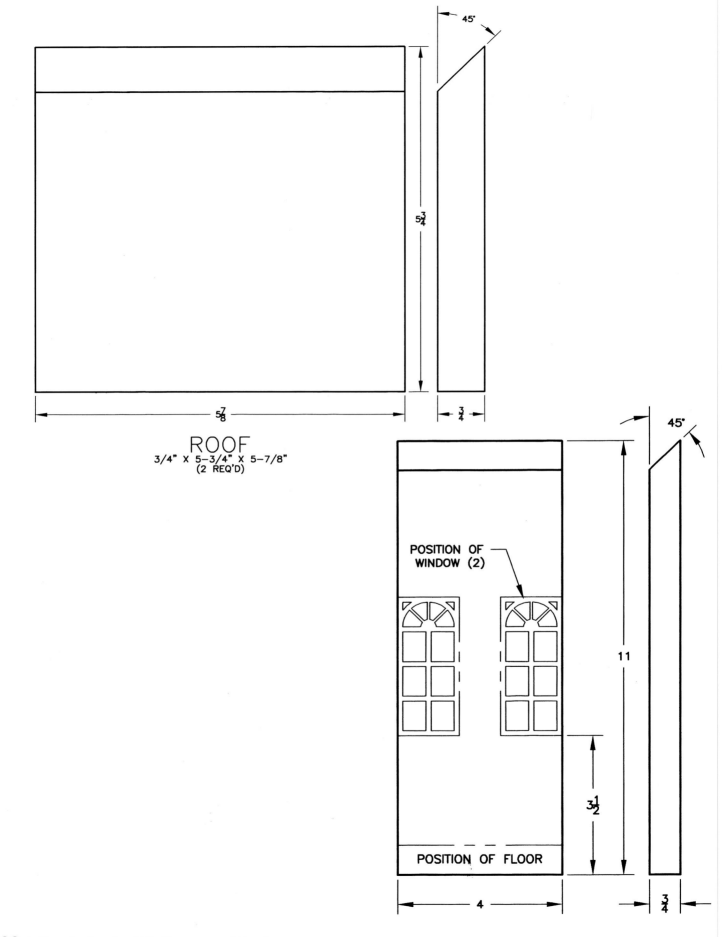

45°

5¾

5⅞

ROOF
3/4" X 5–3/4" X 5–7/8"
(2 REQ'D)

¾

45°

POSITION OF
WINDOW (2)

11

3½

POSITION OF FLOOR

4

¾

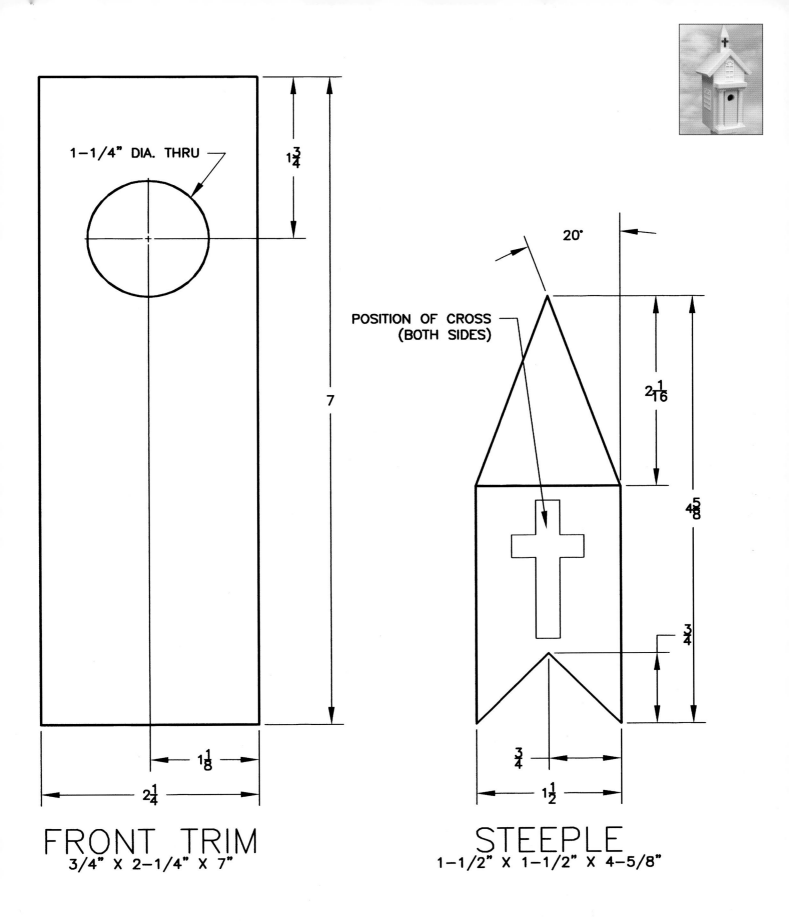

1-1/4" DIA. THRU

$1\frac{3}{4}$

7

$1\frac{1}{8}$

$2\frac{1}{4}$

FRONT TRIM
3/4" X 2-1/4" X 7"

POSITION OF CROSS
(BOTH SIDES)

20°

$2\frac{1}{16}$

$4\frac{5}{8}$

$\frac{3}{4}$

$\frac{3}{4}$

$1\frac{1}{2}$

STEEPLE
1-1/2" X 1-1/2" X 4-5/8"

Country Cottage Birdhouse

The dictionary defines "cottage" as a house at a resort or in the country, used for vacation or as a summer home. This birdhouse is my idea of a cottage. It is a fairly basic design. Simple decorations, such as the chimney, the window dormers and the lattice trellis on each side, give it a sort of country charm.

I chose white and blue for the color scheme. The ¼" holes in the back are air vents. Attach the front piece with screws so it can be removed for cleaning. The Chimney Back piece extends below the rest of the structure to provide a place for attaching the birdhouse to a post. You might even make this piece a few inches longer to give yourself a little more room for the mounting screws.

COUNTRY COTTAGE BIRDHOUSE: PLAN OF PROCEDURE

Construction of the basic house is made from 1x8 pine boards. The Door and the Lattice pieces are cut from ¼"exterior plywood.

The Window Dormers are 1½" wide, the same width as a piece of 2x4. The drawings include both a front and side view of the Window Dormers. To make these, first rip a 14" length of 2x4 to 2¼" wide. Next, cut the 45-degree chamfers. Now lay the piece on its side and cut the 45-degree slant on the back. The piece will be long enough to make all four Window Dormers.

Front and Back: Lay out and cut to size from ¾" stock. Drill the 1¼"-diameter hole through on the Front piece only. Drill the ¼" diameter vent holes on the Back piece.

Side: Lay out and cut to size from ¾" stock. Cut the 45-degree bevel. (Two Pieces Required)

Chimney: Lay out and cut to size from ¾" stock.

Chimney Top: Lay out and cut to size from ¾" stock.

Door: Lay out and cut to size from ¼" stock. Drill the 1¼" diameter hole.

Lattice: Transfer the pattern to ¼" stock and cut out. (Two Pieces Required)

Window Dormer: Lay out and cut to size from 1½" stock. (Four Pieces Required)

Roof #1 and #2: Lay out and cut to size from ¾" stock according to dimensions given in the Bill of Materials.

Chimney Back: Lay out and cut to size from ¾" stock.

Floor: Lay out and cut to size from ¾" stock. Cut the 45-degree angles to allow for drainage.

FINAL ASSEMBLY:

Step 1: Assemble the Sides and the Floor with the Back where shown. Attach the Roof pieces to the Sides and the Back. The back edges of the Roof overlap the Back by ¾".

Step 2: Attach the Front to the Sides with wood screws. (Do not glue in place to allow for later removal when cleaning). Attach the Chimney Back to the Back. Attach the Chimney Top and Chimney to the Roof pieces. Attach the Lattice pieces to the Sides where shown. Attach the Door to the Front where shown.

Step 3: Mount the finished project to a tree or a post.

Paint: Paint the project as desired after assembly. Acrylic latex primer and gloss or semi-gloss exterior acrylic latex paint are recommended. I used winter white, crimson red and sky blue.

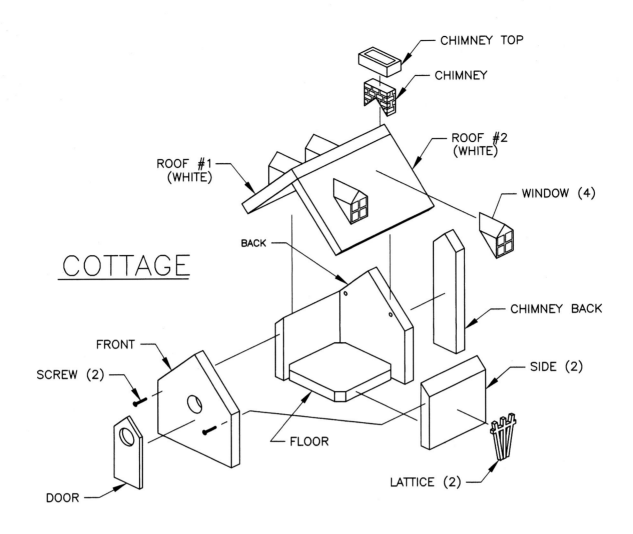

COTTAGE

COUNTRY COTTAGE BIRDHOUSE: BILL OF MATERIALS

Quantity	Description	Size of Material
1	Front	¾" x 6½" x 7¼"
1	Back	¾" x 6½" x 7¼"
2	Side	¾" x 4¾" x 5"
1	Chimney	¾" x 1¾" x 2"
1	Chimney Top	¾" x 1¼" x 2½"
1	Door	¼" x 2¼" x 5"
2	Lattice	¼" x 2" x 3"
4	Window Dormers	1½" x 2¼" x 2¼"
1	Roof #1	¾" x 6¼" x 8¼" (not drawn)
1	Roof #2	¾" x 5½" x 8¼" (not drawn)
1	Chimney Back	¾" x 2" x 8⅝"
1	Floor	¾" x 5" x 5"

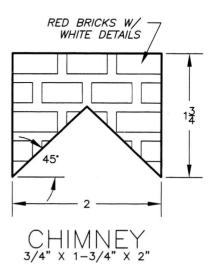

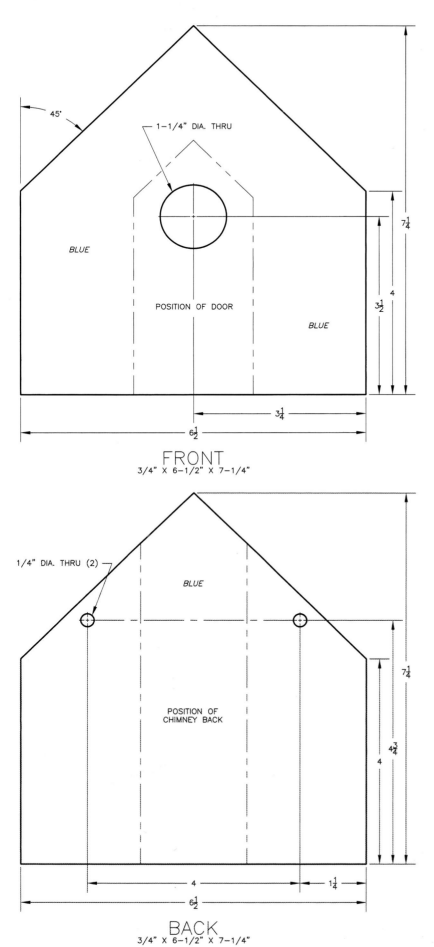

FRONT
3/4" X 6-1/2" X 7-1/4"

45°

1-1/4" DIA. THRU

BLUE

POSITION OF DOOR

BLUE

7 1/4

4

3 1/2

3 1/4

6 1/2

CHIMNEY
3/4" X 1-3/4" X 2"

RED BRICKS W/
WHITE DETAILS

45°

1 3/4

2

CHIMNEY TOP
3/4" X 1-1/4" X 2-1/2"

WHITE

BLACK

WHITE

1 1/4

2 1/2

BACK
3/4" X 6-1/2" X 7-1/4"

1/4" DIA. THRU (2)

BLUE

POSITION OF
CHIMNEY BACK

7 1/4

4 3/4

4

4

1 1/4

6 1/2

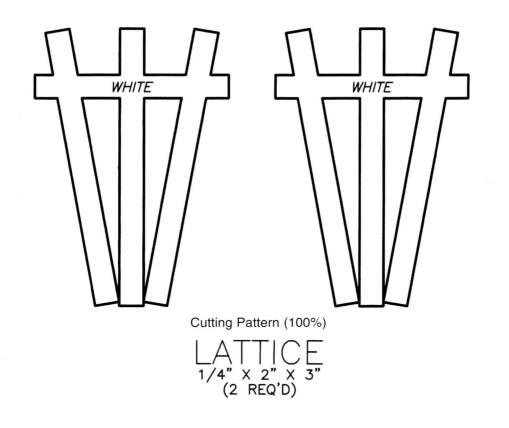

Cutting Pattern (100%)

LATTICE
1/4" X 2" X 3"
(2 REQ'D)

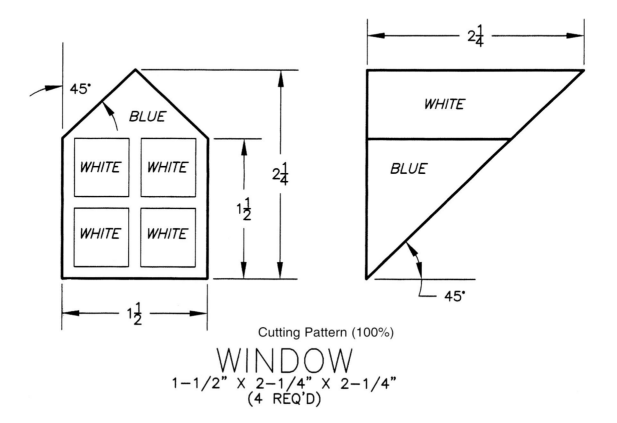

Cutting Pattern (100%)

WINDOW
1–1/2" X 2–1/4" X 2–1/4"
(4 REQ'D)

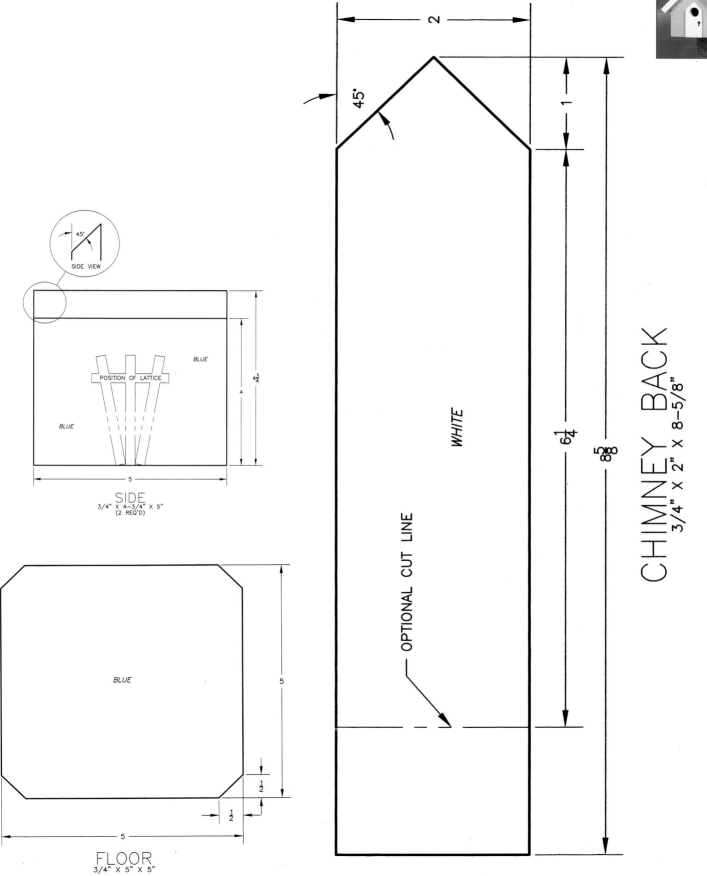

SIDE VIEW

45°

SIDE
3/4" X 4–3/4" X 5"
(2 REQ'D)

BLUE

POSITION OF LATTICE

BLUE

4

4 3/4

5

FLOOR
3/4" X 5" X 5"

BLUE

5

5

1/2

1/2

CHIMNEY BACK
3/4" X 2" X 8–5/8"

2

45°

1

WHITE

6 1/4

5 8/8

OPTIONAL CUT LINE

Gardener's Birdhouse

This birdhouse is identical in size and style to the Country Cottage Birdhouse (page 40) and the Log Cabin Birdhouse (page 52); but, because of the way it has been decorated, it takes on an appearance and personality all its own. It would be fair to say that the birds "fly in the window," as there are window shutters on each side of the entrance hole. A Flower box is attached below the entrance hole.

Decorative Hedges are cut for the Front and both Sides. Although not pictured, there is nothing stopping you from adding the Window Dormers (similar to those shown on the Country Cottage Birdhouse project) to the roof of this house if you want.

PLAN OF PROCEDURE

Construction of the basic house is from 1x8 pine boards. The Doors, Shutters, Flower Bed, Front and Side Hedges are all cut from ¼" exterior plywood.

Separate drawings are not provided for the Back, Floor, Chimney or the Chimney Back pieces, because these pieces are identical to those used on the Country Cottage Birdhouse. Refer to that chapter (page 40) when making these pieces. The Roof #1 and #2 pieces are not drawn, because they are both simple rectangular pieces of wood. Cut them to the size given in the Bill of Materials.

Front and Side Hedge: Transfer the patterns onto ¼" stock and cut one Front and four Side Hedge pieces.

Door, Shutter and Flower Bed: Layout the patterns on ¾" stock and cut two Doors, two Shutters, and one Flower Bed.

Front and Back and Floor: Layout and cut to size from ¾" stock. Drill the 1¼" diameter hole in the Front piece only. The back piece and the floor are identical to those in the Country Cottage Birdhouse project.)

Side: Layout and cut two pieces to size from ¾" stock. Cut the 45-degree bevel.

Chimney and Chimney Back: Make the Chimney as shown in the Country Cottage Birdhouse project.

Roof #1 and #2: Layout and cut to size from ¼" stock according to the dimensions given in the Bill of Materials.

FINAL ASSEMBLY

Assemble the Sides and Floor with the Back as shown. Attach the Roof pieces to the Sides and Back. Attach the Front to the Side with screws. (Do not glue these in place to allow for later disassembly for cleaning). Attach the Chimney Back to the Back. Attach the Chimney to the Roof pieces. Attach the Side Hedges and Door pieces to the Sides where shown. Attach the Front Hedge, Shutter and Flower Bed to the Front where shown.

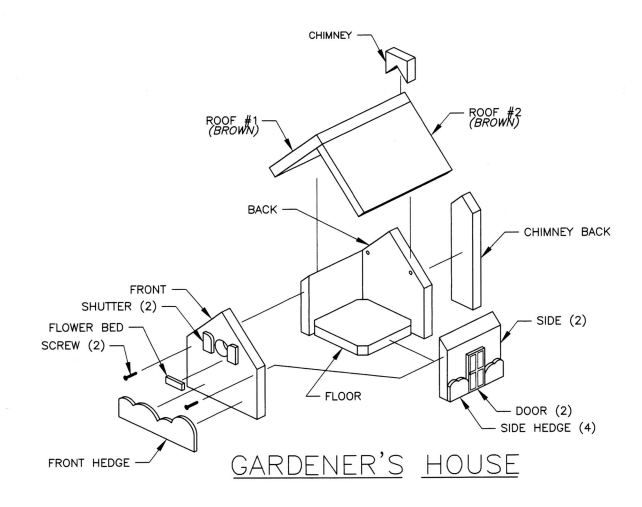

CHIMNEY

ROOF #1 (BROWN)

ROOF #2 (BROWN)

BACK

CHIMNEY BACK

FRONT

SHUTTER (2)

FLOWER BED

SCREW (2)

SIDE (2)

DOOR (2)

SIDE HEDGE (4)

FLOOR

FRONT HEDGE

GARDENER'S HOUSE

GARDENER'S HOUSE: BILL OF MATERIALS

Quantity	Description	Size of Material
1	Front Hedge	¼" x 2⅝" x 7
4	Side Hedge	¼" x 1½" x 1¾"
2	Door	¼" x 1½" x 3
2	Shutter	¼" x ¾" x 1⅜"
1	Flower Bed	¼" x ½" x 1½"
2	Front & Back	¾" x 6½" x 7¼"
2	Side	¾" x 4¾" x 5"
1	Chimney	¾" x 1¾" x 2"
1	Roof #1	¾" x 6¼" x 8¼" (not drawn)
1	Roof #2	¾" x 5½" x 8¼" (not drawn)
1	Floor	¾" x 5" x 5"
1	Chimney Back	¾" x 2 x 8⅝"

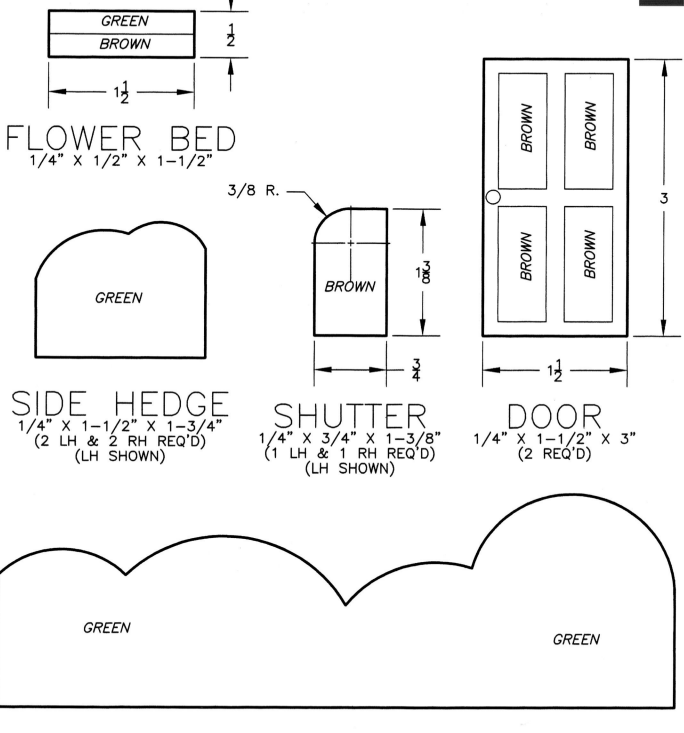

FLOWER BED
1/4" X 1/2" X 1–1/2"

GREEN

BROWN

SIDE HEDGE
1/4" X 1–1/2" X 1–3/4"
(2 LH & 2 RH REQ'D)
(LH SHOWN)

GREEN

SHUTTER
1/4" X 3/4" X 1–3/8"
(1 LH & 1 RH REQ'D)
(LH SHOWN)

BROWN

3/8 R.

DOOR
1/4" X 1–1/2" X 3"
(2 REQ'D)

BROWN BROWN

BROWN BROWN

FRONT HEDGE
1/4" X 2–5/8" X 7"

GREEN

GREEN

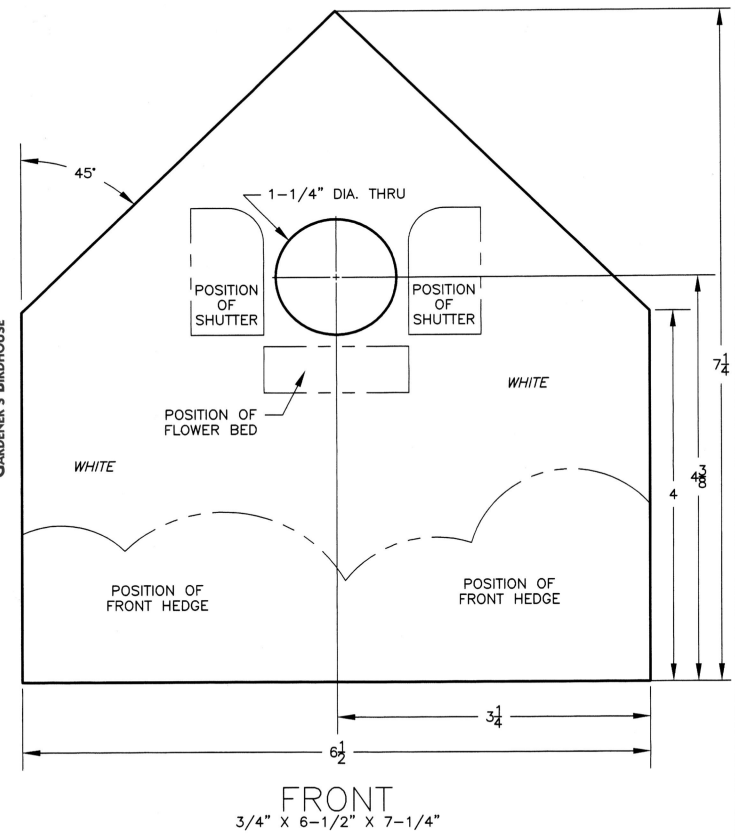

45°

1−1/4" DIA. THRU

POSITION
OF
SHUTTER

POSITION
OF
SHUTTER

WHITE

POSITION OF
FLOWER BED

WHITE

POSITION OF
FRONT HEDGE

POSITION OF
FRONT HEDGE

$7\frac{1}{4}$

$4\frac{3}{8}$

4

$3\frac{1}{4}$

$6\frac{1}{2}$

FRONT
3/4" X 6−1/2" X 7−1/4"

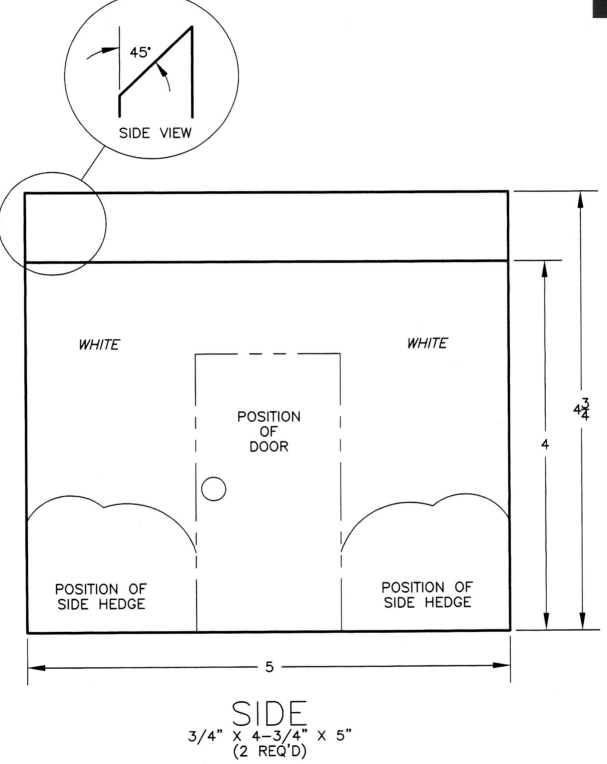

45°

SIDE VIEW

WHITE

POSITION
OF
DOOR

WHITE

POSITION OF
SIDE HEDGE

POSITION OF
SIDE HEDGE

4$\frac{3}{4}$

4

5

SIDE
3/4" X 4-3/4" X 5"
(2 REQ'D)

Log Cabin Birdhouse

Because birdhouses are often placed in wooded areas, it just seemed natural to me that I include a design for a log cabin.

The main structure of this house is identical to the Country Cottage Birdhouse also featured in this book. The main difference is that I attached half dowels to the outside of the structure. I don't recommend trying to cut wood dowel rods in half, as this is dangerous. It is best to simply purchase pre-cut half round dowels. (See Appendix.)

By the way, the window dormers from the Country Cottage Birdhouse project will also fit beautifully on this house if you decide to add even more decoration.

I think this project looks great painted in green and brown.

PLAN OF PROCEDURE

All parts of this project can be cut from 1x8 boards (except for the half round dowels). Drawings for the Roof pieces are not included because they are simple rectangular-shaped pieces.

Separate drawings are not provided for the Back, Floor, Chimney or the Chimney Back pieces, because these pieces are identical to those used on the Country Cottage Birdhouse. Refer to that chapter (page 40) when making these pieces.

You will need a total of seven 16" half round dowels. Cut these to the length given in the Bill of Materials. Attach them with water-resistant glue.

Front and Back: Lay out and cut to size from ¾" stock. Drill the 1¼" diameter hole through on the Front piece only. The back piece is identical to the front piece except for the entrance hole.

Side: Lay out and cut to size from ¾" stock. Cut the 45-degree bevel. (Two Pieces Required)

Chimney: Lay out and cut to size from ¾" stock.

Floor: Lay out and cut to size from ¾" stock. Cut the 45-degree angles to allow for drainage.

Roof #1 and #2: Lay out and cut to size from ¾" stock according to the dimensions given in the Bill of Materials.

Chimney Back: Lay out and cut to size from ¾" stock.

Half Round Dowel #1 and #2: Cut to length from Half Round Dowel stock according to the dimensions given in the Bill of Materials.

FINAL ASSEMBLY:

Step 1: Assemble the Sides and the Floor with the Back where shown. Attach the Roof to the Sides and Back. The back edge of the Roof overlaps the Back by ¾". Attach the Front to the Sides with screws. (Do not glue in place to allow for later removal when cleaning.) Attach the Chimney Back to the Back. Attach the Chimney to the Roof. Attach the Half Round Dowel #2 to the Sides where shown. Attach the Half Round Dowel #1 to the Front where shown.

Step 2: Mount the finished project to a tree or a post.

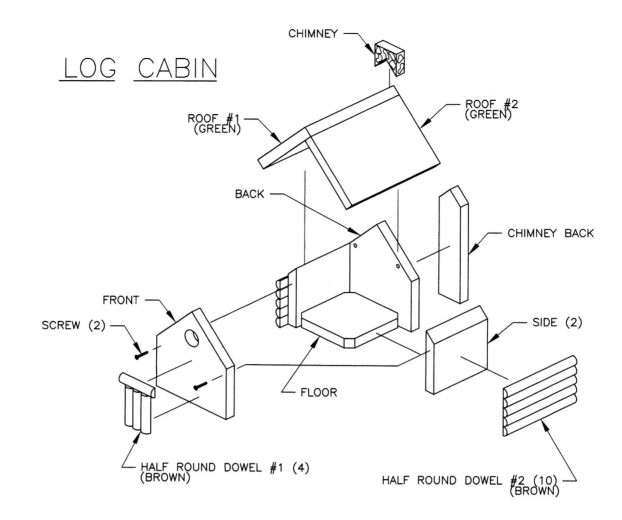

LOG CABIN

CHIMNEY

ROOF #1 (GREEN)

ROOF #2 (GREEN)

BACK

CHIMNEY BACK

FRONT

SCREW (2)

SIDE (2)

FLOOR

HALF ROUND DOWEL #1 (4) (BROWN)

HALF ROUND DOWEL #2 (10) (BROWN)

Log Cabin Birdhouse: Bill of Materials

Quantity	Description	Size of Material
1	Front	¾" x 6½" x 7¼"
1	Back	¾" x 6½" x 7¼"
2	Side	¾" x 4¾" x 5"
1	Roof #1	¾" x 6¼" x 8¼" (not drawn)
1	Roof #2	¾" x 5½" x 8¼" (not drawn)
1	Chimney	¾" x 1¾" x 2"
1	Floor	¾" x 5" x 5"
1	Chimney Back	¾" x 2" x 8⅝"
4	*Half Round Dowel #1 (#8487)	⅜" x ¾" x 3"
10	*Half Round Dowel #2 (#8487)	⅜" x ¾" x 6½"

*Available from Meisel Hardware Specialties.

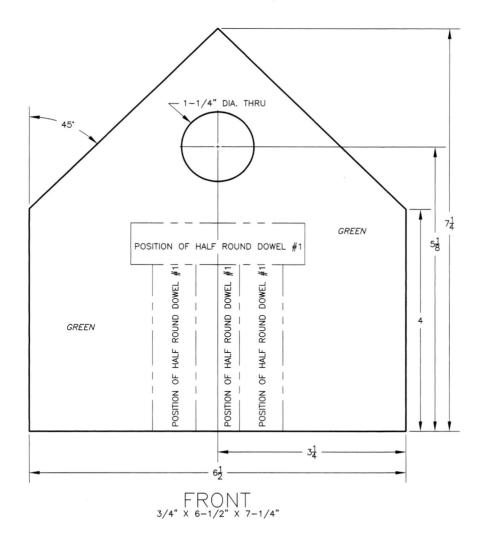

FRONT
3/4" X 6-1/2" X 7-1/4"

1-1/4" DIA. THRU

45°

GREEN

GREEN

POSITION OF HALF ROUND DOWEL #1

POSITION OF HALF ROUND DOWEL #1

POSITION OF HALF ROUND DOWEL #1

POSITION OF HALF ROUND DOWEL #1

$7\frac{1}{4}$

$5\frac{1}{8}$

4

$3\frac{1}{4}$

$6\frac{1}{2}$

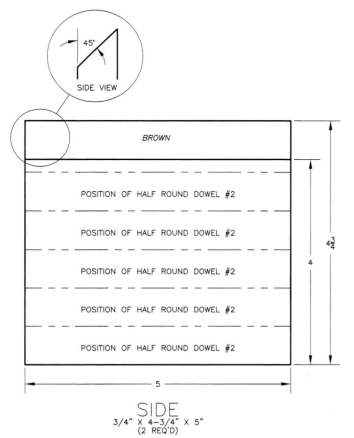

45°

SIDE VIEW

BROWN

POSITION OF HALF ROUND DOWEL #2

POSITION OF HALF ROUND DOWEL #2

POSITION OF HALF ROUND DOWEL #2

POSITION OF HALF ROUND DOWEL #2

POSITION OF HALF ROUND DOWEL #2

$4\frac{3}{4}$

4

5

SIDE
3/4" X 4-3/4" X 5"
(2 REQ'D)

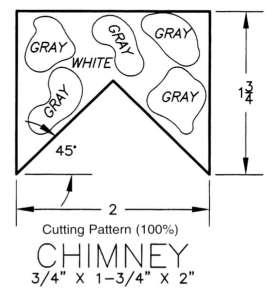

GRAY

GRAY

GRAY

WHITE

GRAY

GRAY

$1\frac{3}{4}$

45°

2

Cutting Pattern (100%)

CHIMNEY
3/4" X 1-3/4" X 2"

Martin Birdhouse

Martins are considered a very desirable bird for a number of reasons. They are fun to watch, they have a unique "morning song" (which you will only hear if you are an early riser), and they consume a vast quantity of insects.

To develop a successful and flourishing martin colony, mount the house on a high pole, at least 12 feet off the ground. Martins love to be around water, although the absence of a nearby pond or lake does not necessarily mean you won't be successful in attracting this bird.

Check your library for books describing techniques for attracting martins. See the Appendix for information on ordering an excellent publication titled *Enjoying Purple Martins*.

PLAN OF PROCEDURE

This house is made primarily from ¼" and ½" exterior plywood. Some pieces, including the Front Steps and Window Boxes, are cut from ¾" solid stock. The Dormers are made by face-gluing three pieces of ¾" stock together. A table saw was used to rip the trim pieces to the length and width specified in the Bill of Materials.

The Side Pieces are hinged on ¼" wood dowels so they can be swung open to provide access for cleaning the house. These pieces are secured at the bottom with screws.

Layout and cut all of the pieces to the sizes as shown on the plans. Drill all holes as required. Finish-sand all parts. The assembly steps refer to the step-by-step illustrations.

Because of the relatively large size of this project, all drawings are to scale. I recommend that you do not try to enlarge these drawings on a photocopier. Instead, use layout tools to transfer the dimensions to the wood.

Step 1: Glue together the Floor, Partitions and one Side as shown. The floor should be ½" from the ends of the Side.

Step 2: Glue the remaining Partitions and Side pieces in place as shown.

Step 3: Fit the Front and Back in place in between the Sides. Drive the ¼" dia. x 1¼" hinge dowels through the ¹⁷⁄₆₄" holes in the Sides into the ¼" holes in the Front and Back. The Front and Back should fit snuggly, yet swing open for cleaning.

Step 4: Glue the Roof pieces to the Sides. Glue the Dormers as shown and glue to the Roof. Glue the Dormer Roofs to the Dormers.

Step 5: Glue the Front Steps to the Front. Glue the Columns in the ½" holes in the Front Steps. Glue the Deck to the Columns and Front. Assemble and glue the Deck Rails and Deck Posts in place as shown.

Step 6: The illustration shows the locations of the Windows and Doors. Mark the locations and paint the areas behind them black. Windows for the Dormers are made by cutting off the top sections of the plastic Windows. Attach the Windows and Doors with the Escutcheon Pins.

Step 7: Glue the Door and House Trim pieces in place.

Step 8: Glue the Window Top Trim, Shutters and Window Boxes in place. The miniature silk flowers are optional. If using these, glue them into the ¹⁄₁₆" holes in the Window Boxes. Install the 1⅝" screws to secure the Front and Back.

Step 9: Glue the Shingles (if used) to the Roofs and Dormer Roofs. Be sure the swinging Front and Back are free to open and shut.

FINAL ASSEMBLY

Paint the birdhouse as desired. Mount the birdhouse with galvanized pipe or PVC pipe and a floor flange or on a sturdy wood post. Mounting height for martins should be 12 to 20 feet. You may wish to drill ¼" drain holes through each of the floors.

Quantity	Part#	Description	Size of Material
2	1	Front and Back	½" x 13¼" x 19⅝"
2	2	Sides	½" x 13¼" x 13"
1	3	Floor	½" x 12¼" x 12¾"
1	4	Partition	¼" x 12¼" x 12¾"
1	5	Partition	¼" x 12¼" x 12⅝"
2	6	Partition	¼" x 6" x 12¾"
1	7	Partition	¼" x 11⅛" x 12¾"
4	8	Hinges	¼" dia x 1¼"
1	9	Roof	½" x 10" x 15¼"
1	10	Roof	½" x 10½" x 15¼"
4	11	Dormer	¾" x 3⅜" x 3⅜"
8	12	Dormer	¾" x 3" x 3"
4	13	Dormer Roof	¼" x 2" x 3⅞"
4	14	Dormer Roof	¼" x 2¼" x 4"
1	15	Front Steps	¾" x 2" x 5"
1	16	Deck	¾" x 2" x 5"
1	17	Deck Rail	¼" x ½" x 5"
2	18	Deck Rails	¼" x ½" x 1½"
11	19	Deck Posts	¼" dia x 1½"
2	20	Columns	½" dia x 6¼"
4	21	House Trim	3⁄16" x ½" x 13"
2	22	Door Top Trim	¼" x ¼" x 2½"
4	23	Door Sides Trim	¼" x ¼" x 4½"
8	24	Window Top Trim	¼" x ¼" x 2"
16	25	Shutters	¼" x ¾" x 3½"
8	26	Window Boxes	¾" x ¾" x 2½"
12	27	*Windows (#8607)	1½" x 3½"
2	28	*Doors (#8606)	2" x 4½"
	29	*Escutcheon Pins (#388)	⅜" x #18
4	30	*Exterior Screws (#1455)	1¼" x #6
		Miniature Silk Flowers (optional)	

*Available from Meisel Hardware Specialties.

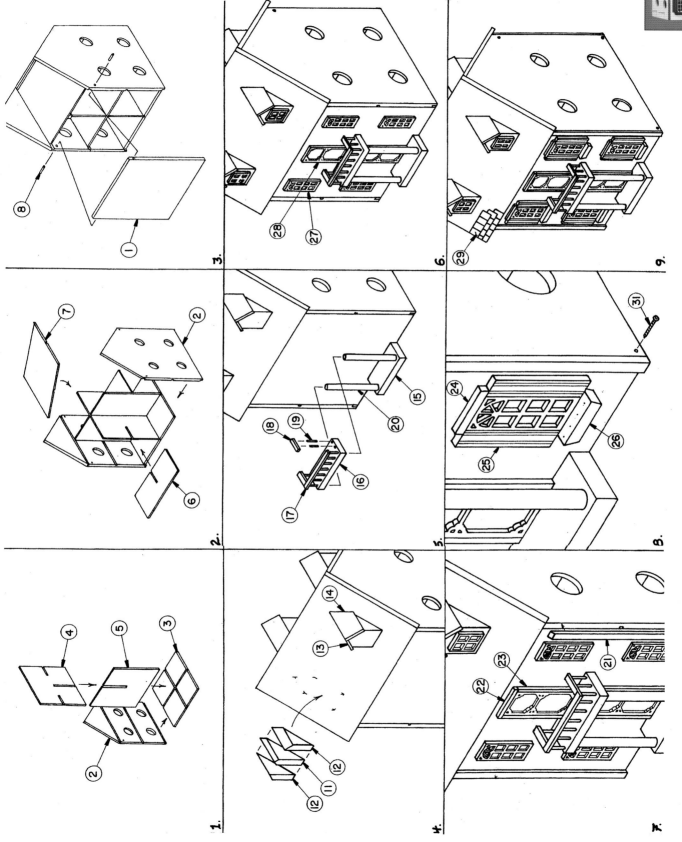

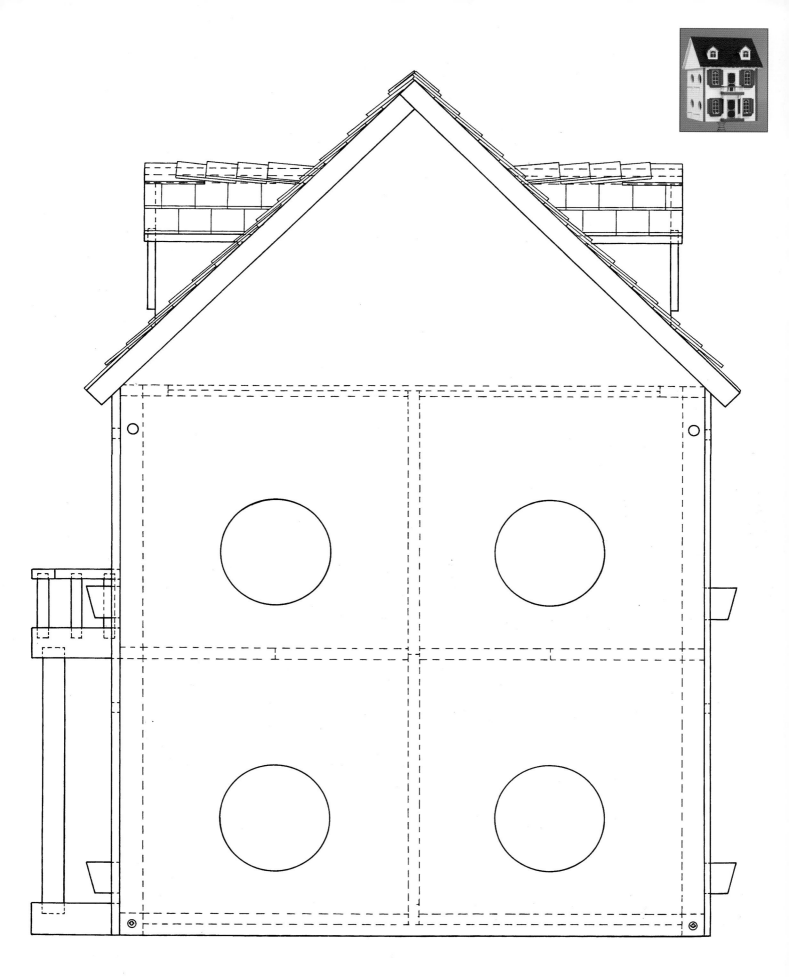

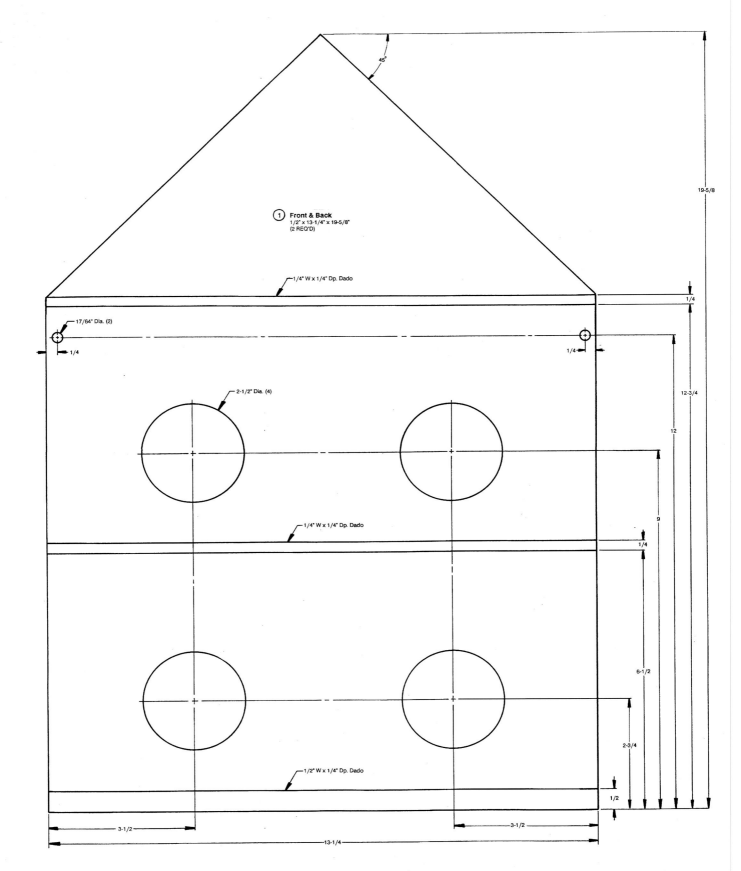

1 **Front & Back**
1/2" x 13-1/4" x 19-5/8"
(2 REQ'D)

45°

19-5/8

1/4" W x 1/4" Dp. Dado

1/4

17/64" Dia. (2)

1/4

1/4

12-3/4

2-1/2" Dia. (4)

12

1/4" W x 1/4" Dp. Dado

1/4

9

6-1/2

1/2" W x 1/4" Dp. Dado

2-3/4

1/2

3-1/2

3-1/2

13-1/4

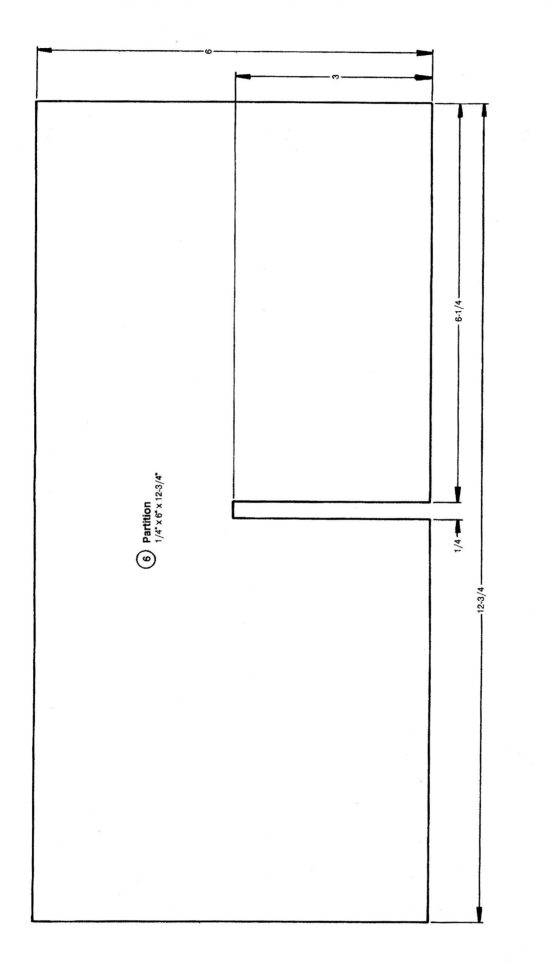

⑥ Partition
1/4" x 6" x 12-3/4"

6

3

6-1/4

1/4

12-3/4

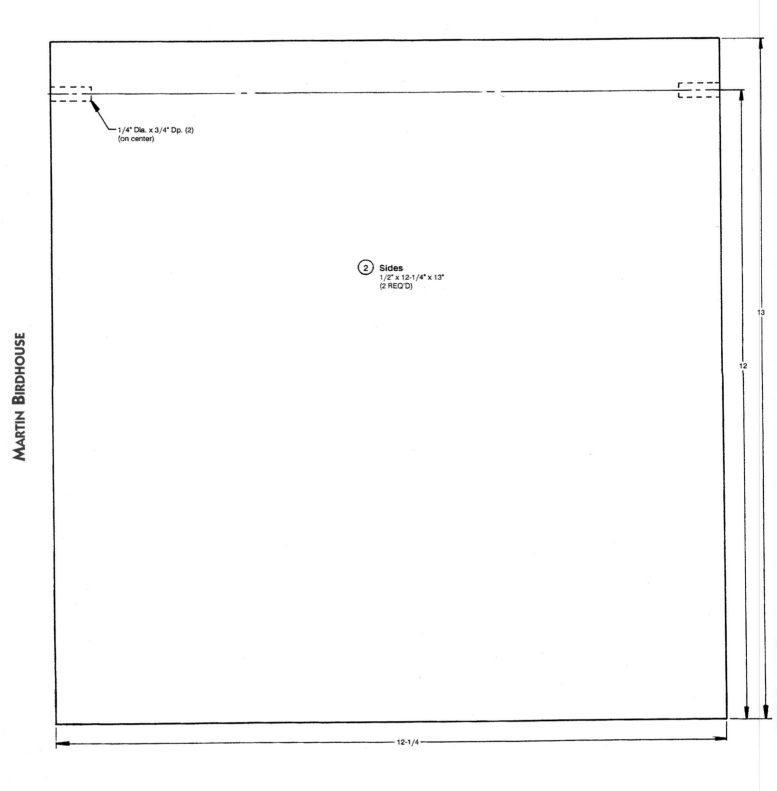

1/4" Dia. x 3/4" Dp. (2)
(on center)

② Sides
1/2" x 12-1/4" x 13"
(2 REQ'D)

13

12

12-1/4

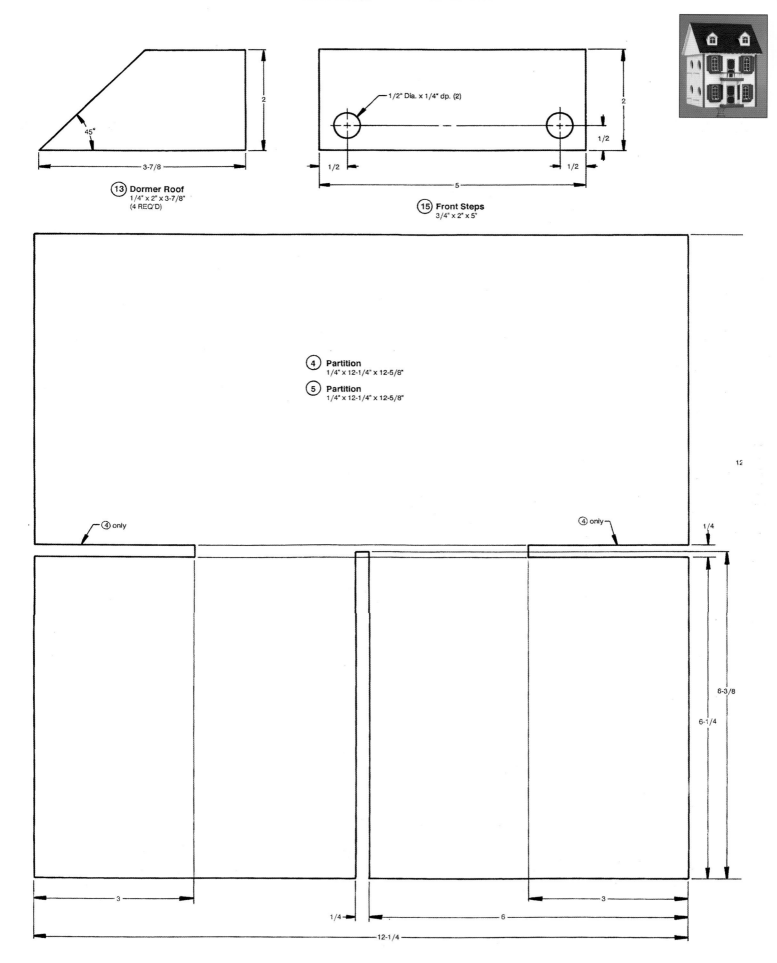

13 **Dormer Roof**
1/4" x 2" x 3-7/8"
(4 REQ'D)

45°

3-7/8

2

1/2" Dia. x 1/4" dp. (2)

15 **Front Steps**
3/4" x 2" x 5"

1/2

2

1/2

5

1/2

4 **Partition**
1/4" x 12-1/4" x 12-5/8"

5 **Partition**
1/4" x 12-1/4" x 12-5/8"

4 only

4 only

1/4

12

6-3/8

6-1/4

3

3

1/4

6

12-1/4

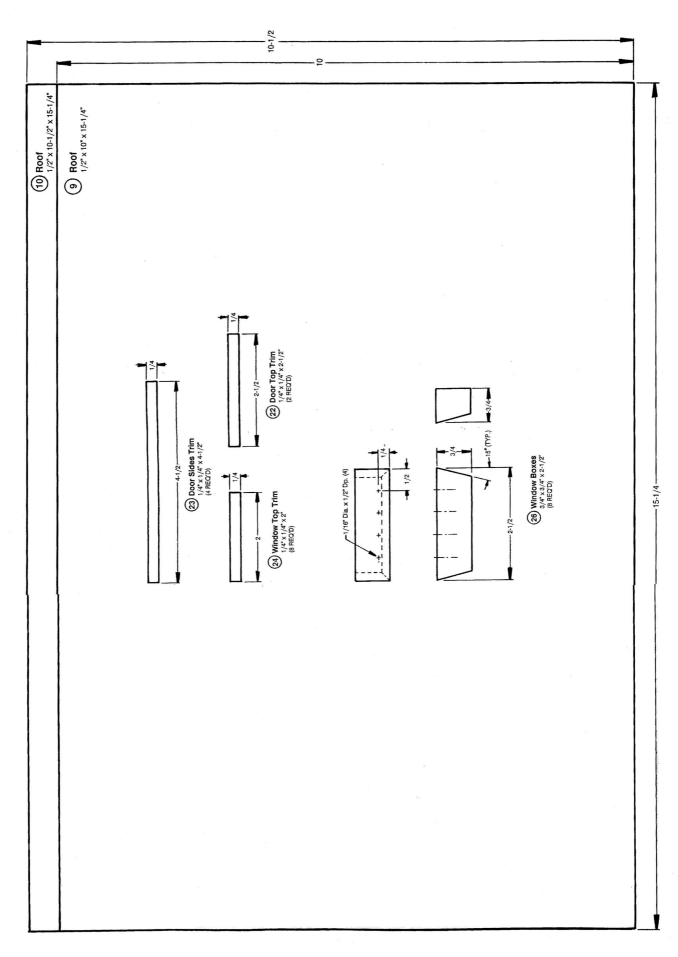

10 Roof
1/2" x 10-1/2" x 15-1/4"

9 Roof
1/2" x 10" x 15-1/4"

22 Door Top Trim
1/4" x 1/4" x 2-1/2"
(2 REQ'D)

23 Door Sides Trim
1/4" x 1/4" x 4-1/2"
(4 REQ'D)

24 Window Top Trim
1/4" x 1/4" x 2"
(8 REQ'D)

26 Window Boxes
3/4" x 3/4" x 2-1/2"
(8 REQ'D)

1/16" Dia. x 1/2" Dp. (4)

15° (TYP.)

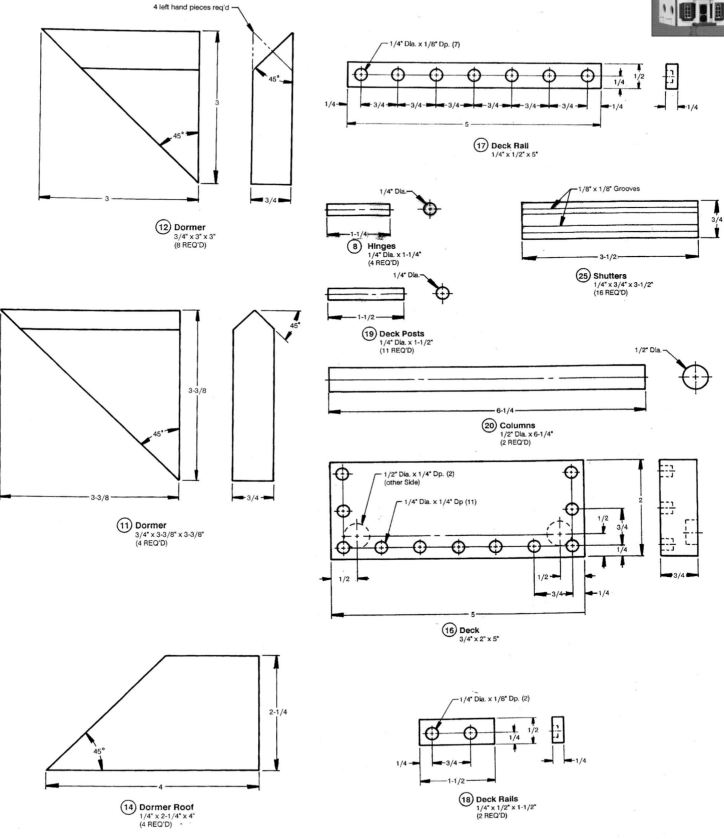

4 left hand pieces req'd

(12) Dormer
3/4" x 3" x 3"
(8 REQ'D)

(11) Dormer
3/4" x 3-3/8" x 3-3/8"
(4 REQ'D)

(14) Dormer Roof
1/4" x 2-1/4" x 4"
(4 REQ'D)

1/4" Dia. x 1/8" Dp. (7)

(17) Deck Rail
1/4" x 1/2" x 5"

1/4" Dia.

(8) Hinges
1/4" Dia. x 1-1/4"
(4 REQ'D)

1/4" Dia.

(19) Deck Posts
1/4" Dia. x 1-1/2"
(11 REQ'D)

1/8" x 1/8" Grooves

(25) Shutters
1/4" x 3/4" x 3-1/2"
(16 REQ'D)

1/2" Dia.

(20) Columns
1/2" Dia. x 6-1/4"
(2 REQ'D)

1/2" Dia. x 1/4" Dp. (2)
(other Side)

1/4" Dia. x 1/4" Dp (11)

(16) Deck
3/4" x 2" x 5"

1/4" Dia. x 1/8" Dp. (2)

(18) Deck Rails
1/4" x 1/2" x 1-1/2"
(2 REQ'D)

Motor Home Birdhouse

Recreational vehicles are becoming ever more popular. Each year more and more people choose them to travel throughout the United States and Canada.

This Motor Home Birdhouse has always been one of my favorites because it is so unique. Design elements, such as the air conditioner on top, the large screw hole buttons for the headlights and, of course, the wooden truck wheels, make it instantly recognizable.

While the project is shown with two compartments, you could leave off the center partition and use only one entrance hole. By making the project with one large cavity and adjusting the size of the entrance hole, this house will accommodate a large variety of different bird species.

PLAN OF PROCEDURE

The Front, Back and Side View Drawings are not drawn full size. You can enlarge these drawings on a photocopier, if desired.

Begin by cutting all pieces to size as given in the Bill of Materials. Assemble the project according to the Exploded Drawings.

The rectangular windows on the Sides and the Front are painted with black paint. The Roof is attached with four Wood Screws (not glue) so it can be removed for cleaning. All lights are made using ⅜" diameter and ⅞" diameter Screw Hole Buttons. Drill ⅜" diameter or ⅞" diameter holes respectively when installing the Screw Hole Buttons. The ten running lights on the top of the project are made

using small Axle Pegs. The 2"-diameter Treaded Wheels are attached with large Axle Pegs. These pegs require ⁵⁄₃₂" and ¹¹⁄₃₂"-diameter mounting holes respectively. The Ladder uses ⅛" diameter x 1⁵⁄₁₆" Dowels for the rungs.

FINAL ASSEMBLY

Step 1: Attach the Back, the Floor, the Partition and the Sides as shown. Attach the Front and Rear Axles to the Floor. Do not attach the Wheels to the Axles and Back with the 2⅜" long Axle Pegs until after the final painting is done.

Step 2: Attach the Hood and the Windshield Header to the Sides. Glue the Windshield to the Hood and Windshield Header from inside the birdhouse. Glue the Front Bumper and the Grill to the Hood. Glue the ⅞" Screw Hole Buttons to the Hood and the ⅜" Screw Hole Buttons to the Front Bumper. Glue the Door to the Side.

Step 3: Attach the Rear Bumper to the Back. Glue the ⅜" Screw Hole Buttons to the Rear Bumper. Assemble the Ladder Sides and ⅛" diameter x 1¹⁵⁄₁₆" Dowels and attach the Ladder Assembly to the Back.

Step 4: Attach the Roof to the Sides with 1¼" Wood Screws. Attach the Air Conditioner to the Roof. Drill the ⁵⁄₃₂" holes for the AP6 Axle Pegs and hammer the Axle Pegs in the Roof.

Motor Home Birdhouse: Bill of Materials

Quantity	Part #	Description	Size of Material
1	#1	Floor	½" x 6" x 14¾"
1	#2	Back	½" x 6" x 6"
2	#3	Side	½" x 6" x 15¹⁵⁄₁₆"
1	#4	Partition	½" x 4¼" x 6"
1	#5	Roof	¾" x 7" x 16"
1	#6	Windshield	½" x 2¾" x 6"
1	#7	Windshield Header	½" x 1⅛" x 7"
1	#8	Hood	½" x 3⅝" x 7"
1	#9	Grill	⅛" x 1½" x 4"
1	#10	Door	⅛" x 2" x 5⅜"
2	#11	Ladder Side	¼" x ¼" x 5½"
1	#12	Air Conditioner	1" x 3" x 3½"
1	#13	Front Bumper	⅜" x ¾" x 7"
1	#14	Rear Bumper	⅜" x ¾" x 7"
1	#15	Front Axle	¾" x 1⅝" x 5½"
1	#16	Rear Axle	¾" x 1⅝" x 4"
4	#17	*Screw Hole Button (#1432)	⅜"
2	#18	*Screw Hole Button (#1437)	⅞"
3	#19	*Treaded Wheel (#7050)	2" dia. x ¾"
2	#20	*Treaded Wheel (#7051)	2" dia. x 1½"
5	#21	*Axle Peg (#AP5)	¹¹⁄₃₂" dia. x 2⅜"
10	#22	*Axle Peg (#AP6)	⁵⁄₃₂" dia. x ⅝"
7	#23	*Dowel (#A35)	⅛" dia. x 1⁵⁄₁₆"
4	#24	*Wood Screw (#WS1148)	1¼" x #8

*Available from Meisel Hardware Specialties.

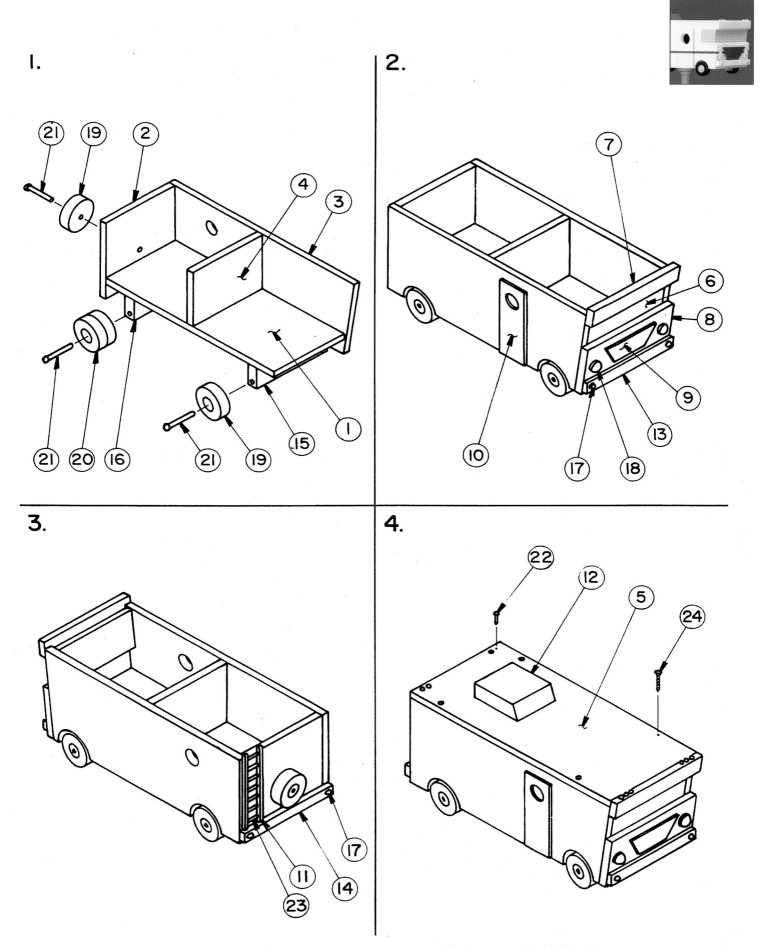

1.

2.

3.

4.

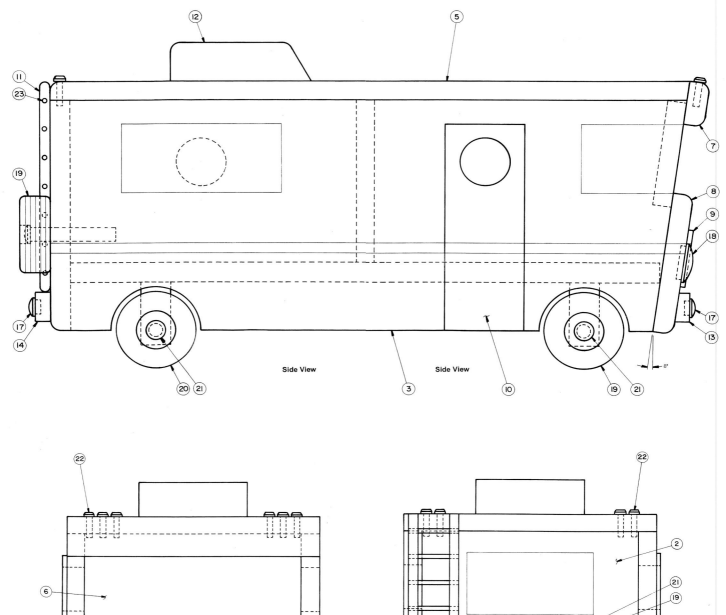

Side View

Side View

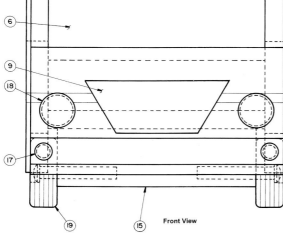

Front View

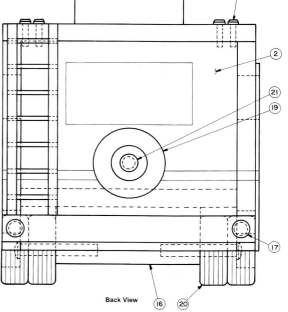

Back View

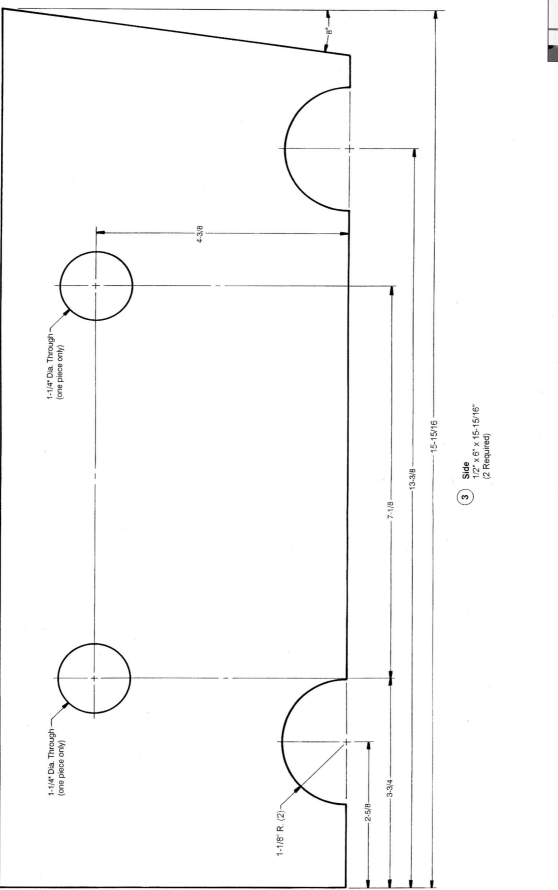

1-1/4" Dia. Through
(one piece only)

1-1/4" Dia. Through
(one piece only)

4-3/8

8°

15-15/16

13-3/8

7-1/8

3-3/4

2-5/8

1-1/8" R. (2)

(3) **Side**
1/2" x 6" x 15-15/16"
(2 Required)

Nesting Shelf Birdhouse

American robins, barn swallows and phoebes won't nest in a traditional birdhouse, but they are likely to build their nests on a nesting shelf. Nesting shelves can be located on the side of your house or garage about 10" down from the eave. Be sure to pick a location that will be protected from raccoons and other predators.

Nesting shelves can be very simple. The ones I design, of course, are not. We all understand that birds can't read. They could care less about my fancy signage. But please remember that the fancy signage isn't added for the sake of the birds. It is added for the sake of humans... humans who have a good sense of humor.

As for the birds, they're just happy to have a sturdy shelf on which to build their nest.

PLAN OF PROCEDURE

This project is constructed primarily from ¾" stock.

Making the Small "Open" Sign and one of the Large Hanging Signs is optional. Several lettering ideas for the Large Sign are provided. Choose only one Large Sign. The lettering on the signs can be transferred with carbon paper or transfer paper. Use a fine point black paint marker to paint the letters.

Mount the finished project by drilling two screw clearance holes in the Back. Screw the project to an outside wall under the eave.

Base: Lay out and cut to size from ¾" stock. Drill the ¼" diameter x ⅜" deep hole.

Back: Lay out and cut to size from ¾" stock.

Side: Lay out and cut to size from ¾" stock. Cut the 30-degree bevel. Transfer the pattern with carbon paper and cut out. Note: There is a right-hand and a left-hand piece.

Roof: Lay out and cut to size from ¾" stock. Cut the 30-degree bevel. (Two Pieces Required)

Roof Trim: Transfer the pattern to ¾" stock and cut out.

Small Sign: Lay out and cut to size from ¾" stock. Drill the ¼" diameter x ⅜" deep hole on center.

Large Sign: Lay out and cut to size from ¾" stock.

Dowel: Cut to 2¾" length from ¼" dowel stock.

FINAL ASSEMBLY:

Step 1: Attach the Sides and the Back to the Base where shown. Attach the Roof to the Sides and Back. Attach the Roof Trim to the Roof approximately ½" from the leading edge. Insert the Dowel in the ¼" hole in the Small Sign and the Base. Insert the Screw Eyes in the Base and the Large Sign where shown. Open the Screw Eyes with pliers, slip the Screw Eyes onto each other and close the Screw Eyes to secure the Large Sign in place.

Step 2: The finished project may be displayed by mounting it with two 1½" x #8 Wood Screws run through shank clearance holes in the Back.

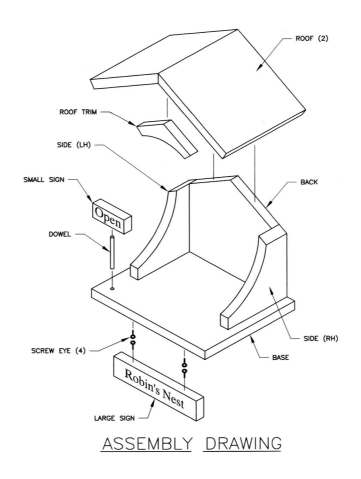

ROOF (2)

ROOF TRIM

SIDE (LH)

SMALL SIGN

Open

DOWEL

BACK

SCREW EYE (4)

Robin's Nest

LARGE SIGN

SIDE (RH)

BASE

ASSEMBLY DRAWING

NESTING SHELF BIRDHOUSE: BILL OF MATERIALS

Quantity	Description	Size of Material
1	Base	¾" x 8¾" x 11"
1	Back	¾" x 8" x 8⁵⁄₁₆"
2	Side	¾" x 5¾" x 6"
2	Roof	¾" x 7⅝" x 7¾"
1	Roof Trim	¾" x 2⅛" x 5¼"
1	Small Sign	¾" x 1¼" x 3"
1	Large Sign	¾" x 1¾" x 8"
1	Dowel	¼" dia. x 2¾"
4	*Screw Eye (#2815)	⁵⁄₁₆" dia. x ¹³⁄₁₆"

*Available from Meisel Hardware Specialties.

Robin's Nest

BASE
3/4" X 8-3/4" X 11"

$8\frac{3}{4}$

1

POSITION OF SIDE (RH)

GREEN

POSITION OF BACK

MOUNT SCREW EYE HERE (2)
(OTHER SIDE)

POSITION OF SIDE (LH)

1/4" DIA. X 3/8" DEEP

GREEN

3

5

11

1

BACK
3/4" X 8" X 8-5/16"

$8\frac{5}{16}$

6

30°

OFF WHITE

OFF WHITE

8

SIDE
3/4" X 5-3/4" X 6"
(1 RH & 1 LH REQ'D)
(RH SHOWN)

6

OFF WHITE

OFF WHITE

$5\frac{3}{4}$

30°

SIDE VIEW

ROOF
3/4" X 7-5/8" X 7-3/4"
(2 REQ'D)

$7\frac{5}{8}$

GREEN

GREEN

$7\frac{3}{4}$

30°

SIDE VIEW

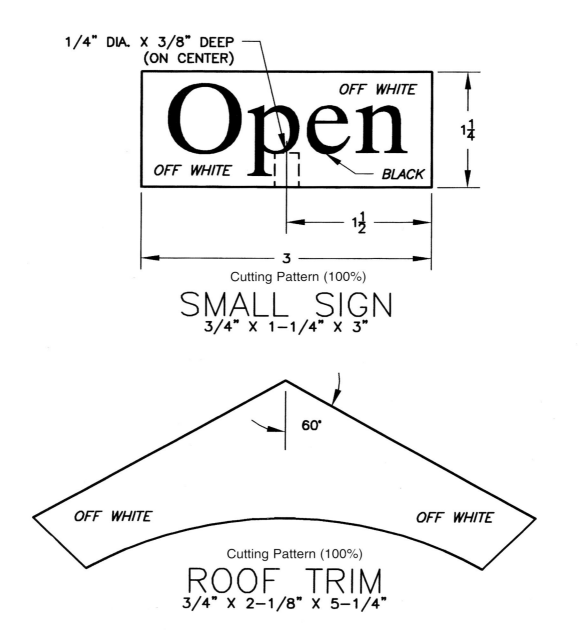

1/4" DIA. X 3/8" DEEP
(ON CENTER)

OFF WHITE

Open

OFF WHITE

BLACK

$1\frac{1}{4}$

$1\frac{1}{2}$

3

Cutting Pattern (100%)

SMALL SIGN
3/4" X 1–1/4" X 3"

60°

OFF WHITE

OFF WHITE

Cutting Pattern (100%)

ROOF TRIM
3/4" X 2–1/8" X 5–1/4"

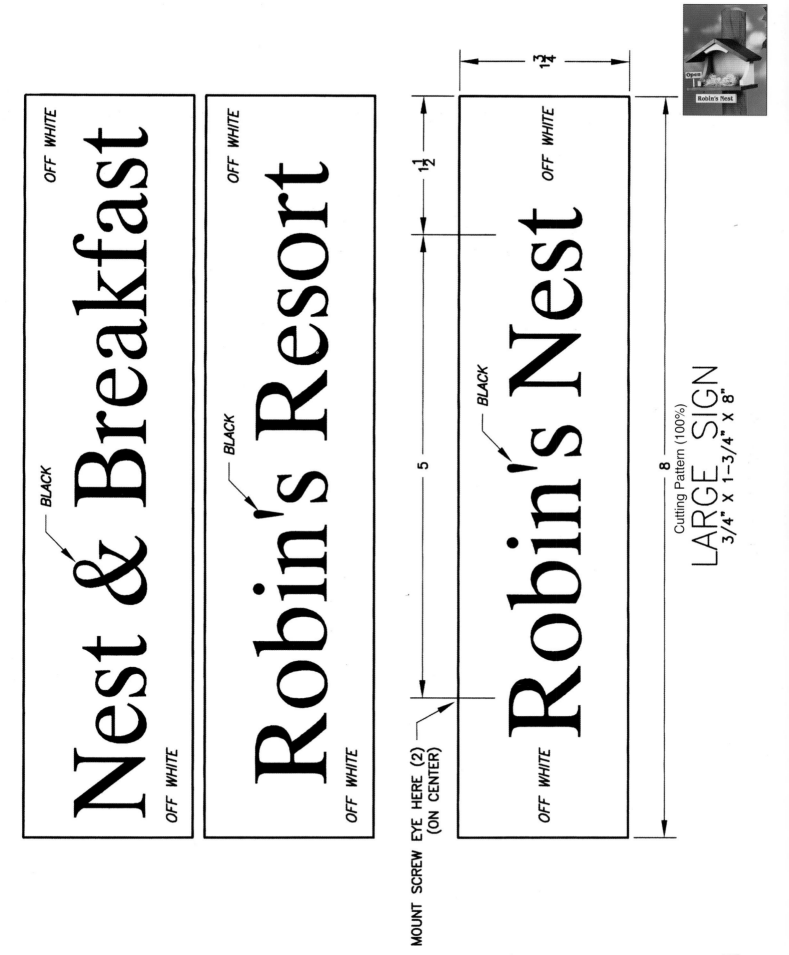

OFF WHITE

BLACK

Nest & Breakfast

OFF WHITE

OFF WHITE

BLACK

Robin's Resort

OFF WHITE

MOUNT SCREW EYE HERE (2)
(ON CENTER)

5

$1\frac{1}{2}$

$1\frac{3}{4}$

BLACK

OFF WHITE

Robin's Nest

OFF WHITE

8

Cutting Pattern (100%)
LARGE SIGN
3/4" X 1–3/4" X 8"

Outhouse Birdhouse

As a child, I was privileged to spend two to three weeks each summer with my grandmother at her lake cabin. It was only about an hour's drive from our home in suburban Minneapolis. Grandma would pick my cousin and me up in her 1956 Chevy. My parents would drive out on weekends.

My grandfather had originally built the cabin in the 1920s. It had an outhouse that was about 150 feet from the cabin, down a narrow trail. My cousin and I called it the "potty house." Every night before bed Grandma would send us out with a flashlight to "do our business." She was always amazed at how quickly we would go and get back. She must not have realized how scary the woods seemed to us at night. We didn't like the mosquitoes either. We sure were glad when Grandma added indoor plumbing.

For some odd reason, outhouses—real ones as well as photographs—have become collectables. I designed this birdhouse for people who have fond memories of outhouses or for people who, for some reason, like to collect them.

PLAN OF PROCEDURE

This project uses ½" plywood for the main structure. Begin by cutting the plywood for the Front, the Back, the Sides, the Roof and the Ground pieces. Cut the top of the Side pieces 15 degrees, as shown in the Side View Drawing.

Cut a 15-degree bevel on the top edge of the Front and the Back pieces. A half pattern of the Ground piece is provided. This is an irregular-shaped piece designed to represent a patch of ground. As an alternative, you may simply cut a rectangular piece of plywood the same size as the bottom of the house (6" x 6¾") and use it in place of the Ground piece.

Attach a plastic Birdhouse Window with ⅜" brass Escutcheon Pins. The Window is surrounded by Trim pieces on the top and bottom, as well as Shutters on each side. The Shutters are ¼" solid wood that has been grooved with a saw blade for decoration.

The door is decorative and is glued to the Front. It is surrounded on the top and sides by Trim. Cut the Trim pieces as well as the Door Handle to the size given in the Bill of Materials. The door hinges are decorative brass Doll House Hinges, attached with ⅛"-long brass pins. Paint this birdhouse before attaching the windows and door hinges. The cedar shakes can be glued on with water-resistant glue.

FINAL ASSEMBLY

Step 1: Attach the Back and the Sides together as shown. Attach the Front to the Sides with the 1¼" wood screws so it can be removed for cleaning. You may want to drill ¼" ventilation holes in the upper part of the Front and the Back. In addition, drill two ¼" drain holes through the Ground piece.

Step 2: Attach the Ground piece to the Sides and Back. (Do not attach to the Front.) Attach the Roof to the Sides and Back. (Do not attach to the Front.) Position the Birdhouse Window and temporarily attach it by driving the ⅜" x #18 Escutcheon Pins about halfway in. Remove the Window after Step #3 to facilitate painting. Glue the Door to the Front.

Step 3: Glue the Door Trim in place around the Door. Glue the Shutters and the Window Trim in place around the Birdhouse Window.

Step 4: Glue the Door Handle to the Door. Glue the Cedar Shakes to the Roof. Then, after painting, nail on the Window and the Door Hinges.

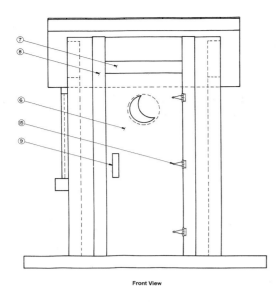

Front View

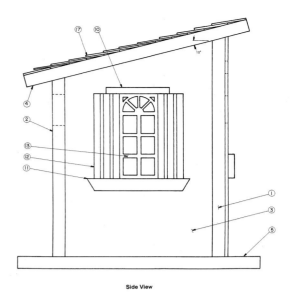

Side View

OUTHOUSE BIRDHOUSE: BILL OF MATERIALS

Quantity	Part #	Description	Size of Material
1	#1	Front	½" x 6" x 9"
1	#2	Back	½" x 6" x 7⁷⁄₁₆"
2	#3	Side	½" x 5¾" x 8⅞"
1	#4	Roof	½" x 7½" x 9"
1	#5	Ground	½" x 9½" x 9½"
1	#6	Door	⅛" x 3" x 7½"
1	#7	Door Trim	⅛" x ½" x 3"
2	#8	Door Trim	⅛" x ½" x 9"
1	#9	Door Handle	¼" x ¼" x 1"
1	#10	Window Trim	¼" x ¼" x 2½"
1	#11	Window Trim	½" x ½" x 4"
2	#12	Shutter	¼" x 1" x 3½"
1	#13	*Birdhouse Window (#8607)	1½" x 3½"
4	#14	*Escutcheon Pin (#388)	⅜" x #18
3	#15	*Doll House Hinge (#6510)	½" x ⁵⁄₁₆"
18	#16	*Escutcheon Pin (#6509)	⅛" x .023"
Misc.	#17	*Cedar Shakes (#7688)	¾" x 1¼"
4	#18	*Wood Screw (#WS1148)	1¼" x #8

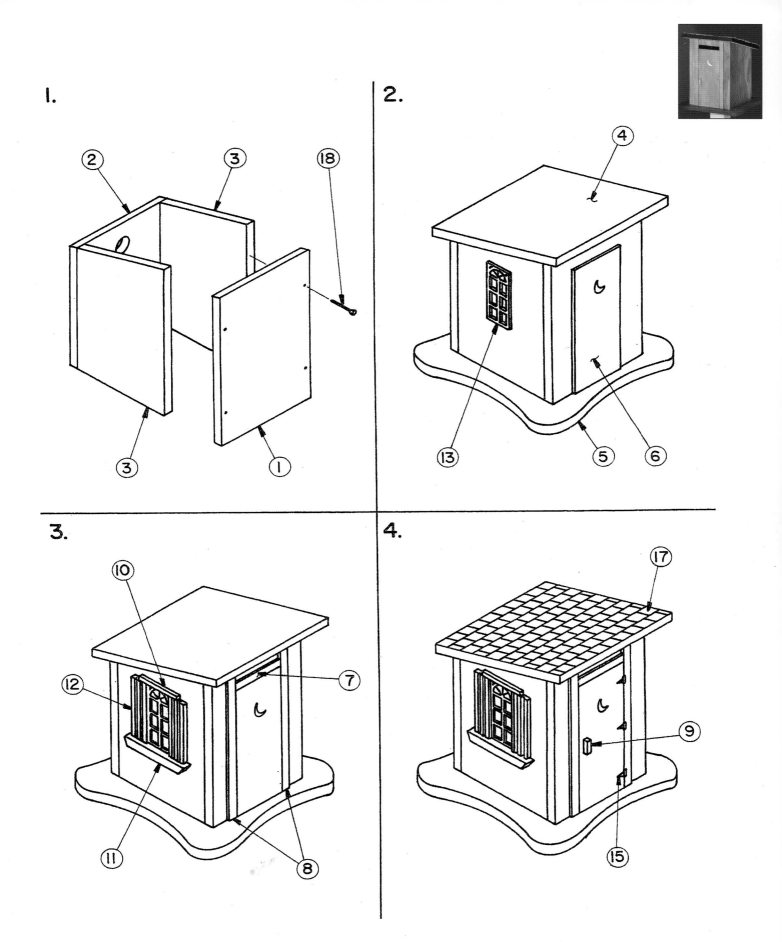

1.

2.

3.

4.

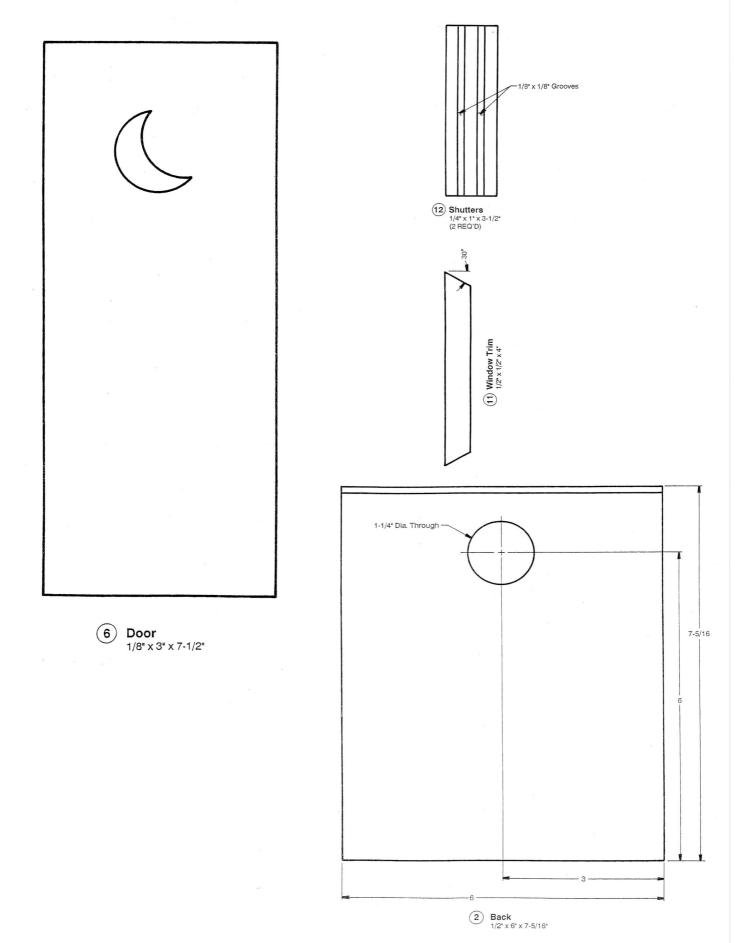

1/8" x 1/8" Grooves

12 Shutters
1/4" x 1" x 3-1/2"
(2 REQ'D)

30°

11 Window Trim
1/2" x 1/2" x 4"

6 Door
1/8" x 3" x 7-1/2"

1-1/4" Dia. Through

7-5/16

6

3

6

2 Back
1/2" x 6" x 7-5/16"

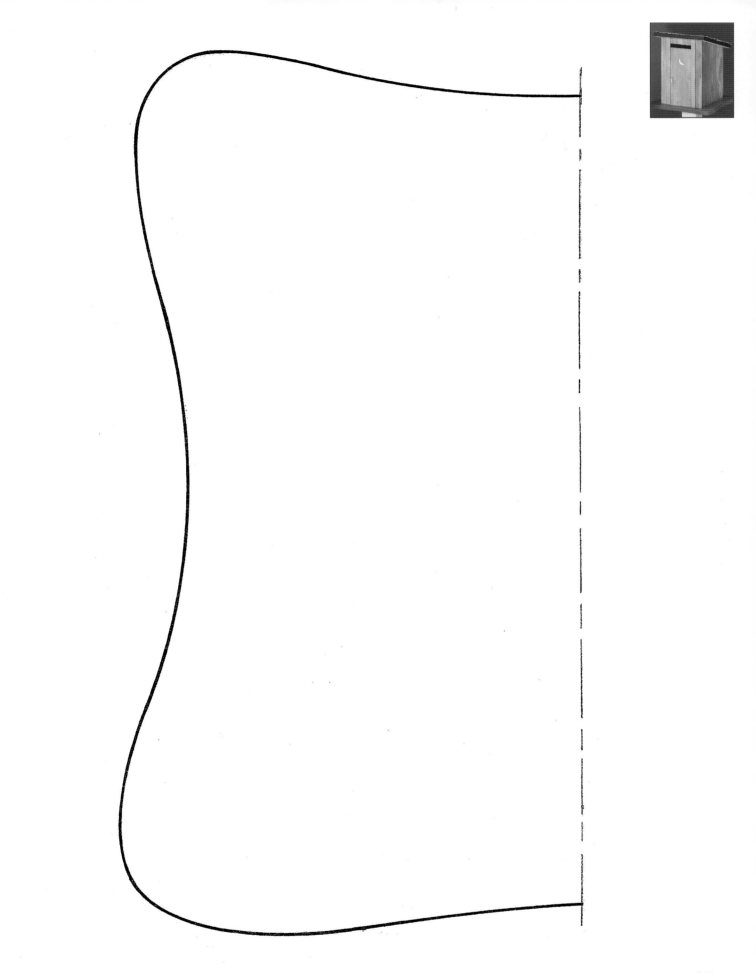

Swinging Cat Birdhouse

This birdhouse can best be described as a comic birdhouse. One of the design challenges was to create something that resembled an animal without making the design too complicated. I wanted a shape that would be simple to cut out and assemble. I also wanted the simplest possible paint job, as not all hobbyists are necessarily skilled at decorative painting. To complete the look of a cat on a swing, this birdhouse is suspended from a tree branch by chains. Ropes can also be used.

PLAN OF PROCEDURE

This project is constructed from ½" exterior plywood and ¾" stock. Waterproof glue is recommended for outdoor use. Joints should be reinforced with nails or screws.

Cat: Enlarge pattern 200% and transfer to ½" stock. Drill the 1⅜" diameter hole and cut out the pattern.

Tail: Enlarge 200% and transfer the pattern to ½" stock. Cut out and drill the ⁷⁄₆₄" diameter x ½" deep pilot holes on center for the 1" screws.

Fingers, Knuckles, Feet and Thumbs: Enlarge the patterns 200% and transfer to ½" stock. Cut out two of each.

Side: Layout and cut to size from ½" stock. Drill the ⁹⁄₆₄" diameter holes and countersink for the ¾" x #6 Wood Screws. Drill two ¼" diameter holes to provide ventilation.

Top: Layout and cut to size from ½" stock. Drill the ⁹⁄₆₄" diameter holes and countersink for the ¾" and 1" x #6 Wood Screws.

Back: Layout and cut to size from ½" stock. Drill the ⁹⁄₆₄" diameter holes and countersink for the ¾" x #6 Wood Screws.

Cleat: Layout and cut to size from ½" stock. Drill the ⁹⁄₆₄" diameter holes though and countersink for the ¾" x #6 Wood Screws.

Bottom: Layout and cut to size from ½" stock. Drill the

⁹⁄₆₄" diameter holes though and countersink for the 1" x #6 Wood Screws.

Swing Seat: Layout and cut to size from ¾" stock. Drill the ⁷⁄₆₄" diameter pilot holes for the 1" x #6 Wood Screws and ⅛" diameter pilot holes for the Screw Eyes.

FINAL ASSEMBLY

Finish-sand all parts. Glue the Knuckles, Thumbs and Feet to the Cat where shown. Glue the Fingers to the Knuckles and Thumbs. Paint the Birdhouse orange to match the Cat. Paint or stain the Swing Seat brown. Paint the Cat and the remaining pieces as shown or as desired with exterior paint. Do not paint the interior of the Birdhouse.

Attach the Cleats to the Sides with the ¾" Wood Screws and glue. Assemble the Top, Bottom and Sides. Position Birdhouse on the Back Side of the Cat as shown by the broken lines, then mount the Birdhouse to the Cat with ¾" Screws through the Cleats. Attach the Tail to the Top with 1" Screws. Attach the Back to the Sides and Bottom of the Birdhouse. Do not glue the Back shut. To clean the birdhouse, remove the bottom ¾" Screw in the Back and swing the Back up.

Attach the Bottom of the Birdhouse to the Swing Seat with 1" Screws then attach the Screw Eyes to the Swing Seat.

Separate the Jack Chain so that you have four 30"-long pieces and two 18"-long pieces. Attach the 30" pieces to the Screw Eyes on the Swing Seat. Pass the front two pieces of Chain through the gaps in the Cat's hands. Open one end of the 18" chains. Loop the open link through the two closed loops of the 30" Chains on the right Side of the Cat and close the loop. Do the same for the Left Side. The ends of the 18" lengths attach to the Screw Eyes for final installation of the Birdhouse.

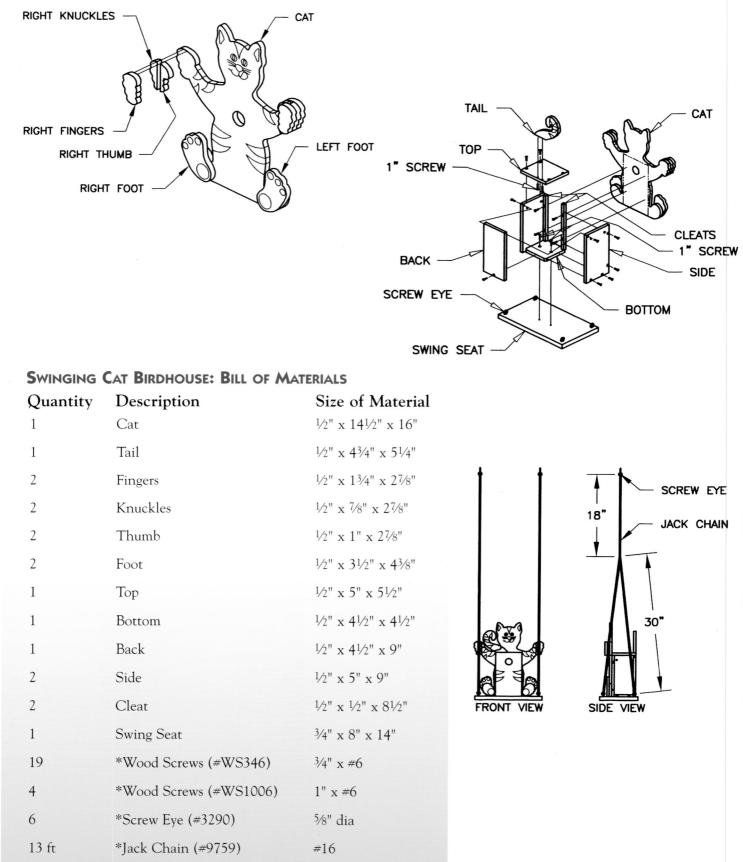

SWINGING CAT BIRDHOUSE: BILL OF MATERIALS

Quantity	Description	Size of Material
1	Cat	½" x 14½" x 16"
1	Tail	½" x 4¾" x 5¼"
2	Fingers	½" x 1¾" x 2⅞"
2	Knuckles	½" x ⅞" x 2⅞"
2	Thumb	½" x 1" x 2⅞"
2	Foot	½" x 3½" x 4⅜"
1	Top	½" x 5" x 5½"
1	Bottom	½" x 4½" x 4½"
1	Back	½" x 4½" x 9"
2	Side	½" x 5" x 9"
2	Cleat	½" x ½" x 8½"
1	Swing Seat	¾" x 8" x 14"
19	*Wood Screws (#WS346)	¾" x #6
4	*Wood Screws (#WS1006)	1" x #6
6	*Screw Eye (#3290)	⅝" dia
13 ft	*Jack Chain (#9759)	#16

*Available from Meisel Hardware Specialties.

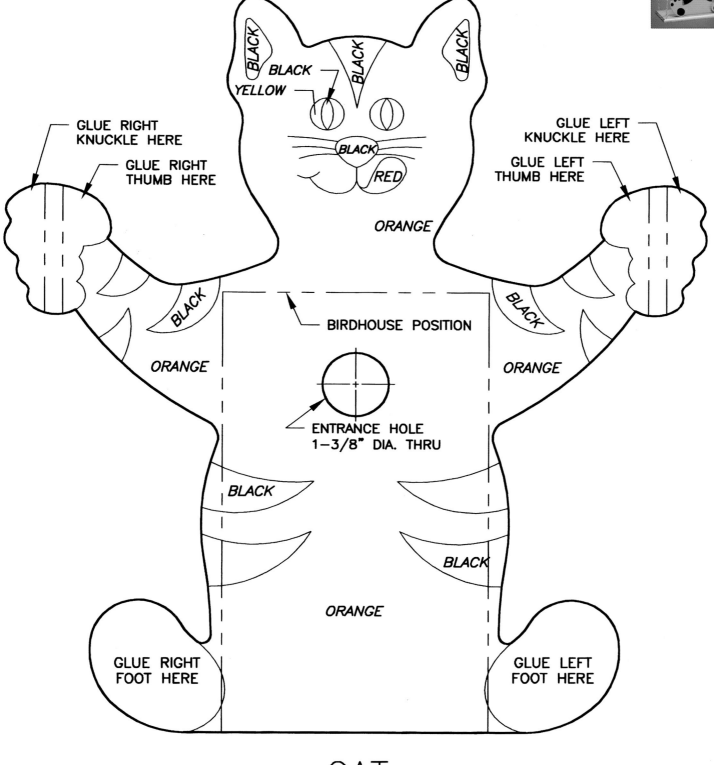

GLUE RIGHT
KNUCKLE HERE

GLUE RIGHT
THUMB HERE

GLUE LEFT
KNUCKLE HERE

GLUE LEFT
THUMB HERE

BLACK

BLACK

BLACK

BLACK

BLACK

YELLOW

BLACK

RED

ORANGE

BLACK

BLACK

ORANGE

ORANGE

BIRDHOUSE POSITION

ENTRANCE HOLE
1–3/8" DIA. THRU

BLACK

BLACK

ORANGE

GLUE RIGHT
FOOT HERE

GLUE LEFT
FOOT HERE

CAT
1/2" X 14–1/2" X 16"

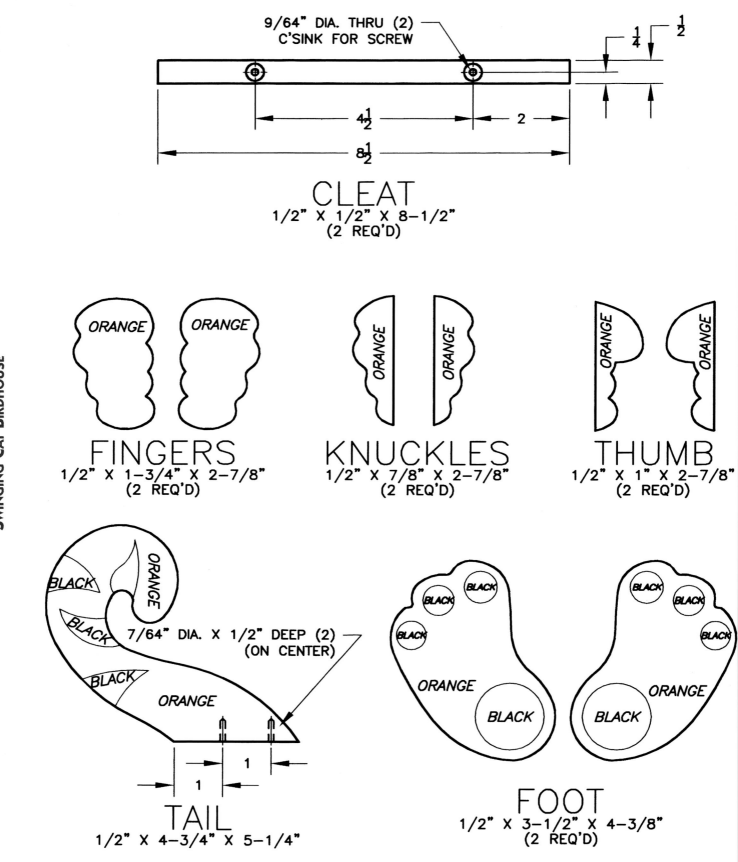

9/64" DIA. THRU (2)
C'SINK FOR SCREW

$4\frac{1}{2}$

2

$8\frac{1}{2}$

$\frac{1}{4}$

$\frac{1}{2}$

CLEAT
1/2" X 1/2" X 8-1/2"
(2 REQ'D)

ORANGE   ORANGE

FINGERS
1/2" X 1-3/4" X 2-7/8"
(2 REQ'D)

ORANGE   ORANGE

KNUCKLES
1/2" X 7/8" X 2-7/8"
(2 REQ'D)

ORANGE   ORANGE

THUMB
1/2" X 1" X 2-7/8"
(2 REQ'D)

BLACK
ORANGE
BLACK
BLACK
ORANGE

7/64" DIA. X 1/2" DEEP (2)
(ON CENTER)

1

1

TAIL
1/2" X 4-3/4" X 5-1/4"

BLACK   BLACK
BLACK   BLACK
BLACK   BLACK
ORANGE   ORANGE
BLACK   BLACK

FOOT
1/2" X 3-1/2" X 4-3/8"
(2 REQ'D)

BOTTOM
1/2" X 4-1/2" X 4-1/2"

9/64" DIA. THRU (2)
C'SINK FOR SCREW

$4\frac{1}{2}$

$2\frac{1}{4}$

$2\frac{1}{2}$ 1

$4\frac{1}{2}$

BACK
1/2" X 4-1/2" X 9"

9/64" DIA. THRU
C'SINK FOR SCREW

ORANGE
(OUTSIDE ONLY)

$4\frac{1}{2}$

$2\frac{1}{4}$

$\frac{1}{4}$

9

TOP
1/2" X 5" X 5-1/2"

1   1

9/64" DIA. THRU (2)
C'SINK FOR SCREW (OTHER SIDE)

MOUNT TAIL HERE

$\frac{1}{4}$

ORANGE
(OUTSIDE ONLY)

9/64" DIA. THRU (4)
C'SINK FOR SCREW

3   5

1

$\frac{1}{4}$ $\frac{1}{4}$

$5\frac{1}{2}$

SIDE
1/2" X 5" X 9"
(2 REQ'D)

$\frac{1}{4}$

$\frac{1}{4}$

ORANGE
(OUTSIDE ONLY)

1

$2\frac{1}{2}$ 5

9/64" DIA. THRU (5)
C'SINK FOR SCREW

3

1/4" DIA. THRU (2)

$\frac{1}{4}$

1

1

$\frac{1}{4}$

6   $1\frac{1}{2}$

9

SWING SEAT
3/4" X 8" X 14"

1/8" DIA. X 1/2" DEEP (4)

7/64" DIA. THRU (2)

$\frac{3}{4}$

8

$4\frac{3}{4}$

$\frac{3}{4}$

BROWN

BROWN

$\frac{3}{4}$

$\frac{3}{4}$

$2\frac{1}{2}$ $5\frac{1}{4}$

14

Three Simple Birdhouses

This book wouldn't be complete if I didn't include several basic birdhouses. These are the projects to choose when you—or possibly your spouse—volunteer to help a group such as a local scout troop build birdhouses.

Here's why these projects work so well. First: readily available materials. All three of these birdhouses are made completely from ¾" boards. Just pick up some 1x8 pine boards at the lumber company. Second: duplication. Because all the pieces can be cut on a table saw, they lend themselves to mass production methods. Third: simplicity. First time builders will have little difficulty understanding how the pieces are assembled because each birdhouse has only a few pieces.

That's not to say that you, as the adult supervisor, won't have to do some planning. Here's what I recommend: Choose only one design and stay with it. Precut all pieces on your table saw. Make enough pieces for each person. Then pre-drill all the holes including holes for the nails. This lets the children know how many nails to use, and exactly where to put them. It also increases the probability that the nails will go in straight.

To get them started, first demonstrate how to glue and nail the first two pieces together. Then pass out only those two pieces and get everyone through their first assembly step. Continue in this manner, piece by piece, until everyone has finished his project. Be sure to have each child write his name on the bottom of his house, as the houses will all look very similar when the children are finished!

PLAN OF PROCEDURE

Because this chapter includes three different birdhouses, each piece is labeled with the name of the birdhouse and #1, #2 or #3. So if you're building the Slant Roof Birdhouse (Birdhouse #1), for example, you would look for those drawings that were labeled Side #1, Roof #1, Floor #1 etc. All pieces for each birdhouse can be cut from 1x8 pine boards.

All parts are drawn to scale. Although you could enlarge the drawings by 200% to make full size patterns, this really isn't necessary. Just use layout tools to transfer the drawings of the pieces to your wood. Of course, even this step can be eliminated by simply setting your table saw to cut the pieces as described on the Bill of Materials. The corners of each of the Floor pieces are cut off to provide for water drainage.

SLANT ROOF BIRDHOUSE (BIRDHOUSE #1)

Roof #1 and Back #1: Layout and cut to size from ¾" stock.

Front #1: Layout and cut to size from ¾" stock. Drill the 1⅛" diameter hole.

Side #1: Layout and cut to size from ¾" stock. Drill the ¼" diameter holes.

Floor #1: Layout and cut to size from ¾" stock. Cut the corners as shown.

FINAL ASSEMBLY

Assemble one of the Sides and the Floor with the Back piece as shown. Attach the Front to the Side and Floor. Attach the Roof to the Side, Front and Back.

The remaining Side swings open for cleaning and should not be glued in place. Fit the remaining Side piece so that it slips into place between the Front and Back. Drive two nails through the Front and Back and into the Side. These nails act as hinges. The Side should fit snug, yet swing open for cleaning. Secure the bottom of the Side piece to the Floor with a screw. To clean the birdhouse, remove the retaining screw and swing the Side open.

QUICK AND EASY BIRDHOUSE (BIRDHOUSE #2)

Roof #2: Layout and cut to size from ¾" stock.

Back #2: Layout and cut to size from ¾" stock. Cut the 30-degree bevel.

Front #2: Layout and cut to size from ¾" stock. Drill the 1⅛" diameter hole. Cut the 30-degree bevel.

Side #2: Layout and cut to size from ¾" stock. Drill the ¼" diameter holes.

Brace #2: Layout and cut to the size given in the Bill of Materials.

Floor #2: Layout and cut to size from ¾" stock. Cut the corners as shown.

Perch #2, Eave #2A & Eave #2B: Layout and cut to size from ¾" stock.

FINAL ASSEMBLY

Glue and nail the Back, the Floor and the Side pieces together. The Front piece hinges at the bottom on two nails. It is held closed at the top by a single screw driven through one of the Side # 2 pieces. You may need to trim up to ¹⁄₁₆" from the width of the Front piece to be sure there is clearance between the Side pieces.

Attach the Eaves and the Perch. Attach the Brace to the back of the project. The purpose of the Brace is to make it easier to mount the birdhouse. The Brace piece extends below the house. Drill two screw clearance holes in the exposed end of the Brace for attachment screws. Attach the Roof.

DIAMOND BIRDHOUSE (BIRDHOUSE #3)

Roof #3A and Roof #3B: Layout and cut to size from ¾" stock.

Floor #3A: Layout and cut to size from ¾" stock. Cut the corner as shown for drainage.

Floor #3B: Layout and cut to size from ¾" stock.

Back #3: Layout and cut to size from ¾" stock.

Front #3: Layout and cut to size from ¾" stock. Drill the 1⅛" diameter hole.

FINAL ASSEMBLY

Assemble the Floor and Roof pieces with the Back as shown. Attach the Front to the Floor pieces with screws as shown. To clean remove the screw and open the Front.

THREE SIMPLE BIRDHOUSES: BILL OF MATERIALS

Quantity	Description	Size of Material
Birdhouse #1		
1	Back #1	¾" x 5½" x 11"
1	Roof #1	¾" x 5½" x 8¼"
1	Front #1	¾" x 5½" x 8"
2	Side #1	¾" x 5½" x 8"
1	Floor#1	¾" x 4" x 5½"
Birdhouse #2		
1	Roof #2	¾" x 7¼" x 8"
2	Side #2	¾" x 5½" x 7½"
1	Front #2	¾" x 4" x 7½"
1	Back #2	¾" x 4" x 4¾"
1	Floor #2	¾" x 4" x 4"
1	Brace #2	¾" x 3½" x 8"
1	Eaves #2 A	¾" x ¾" x 1¾"
1	Eaves #2 B	¾" x ¾" x 2½"
1	Perch #2	¾" x ¾" x 2½"
Birdhouse #3		
1	Roof #3 A	¾" x 6½" x 7¼"
1	Roof #3 B	¾" x 5¾" x 7¼"
1	Floor #3 A	¾" x 4¼" x 5½"
1	Floor #3 B	¾" x 5" x 5½"
1	Front #3	¾" x 5" x 5"
1	Back #3	¾" x 4¼" x 4¼"

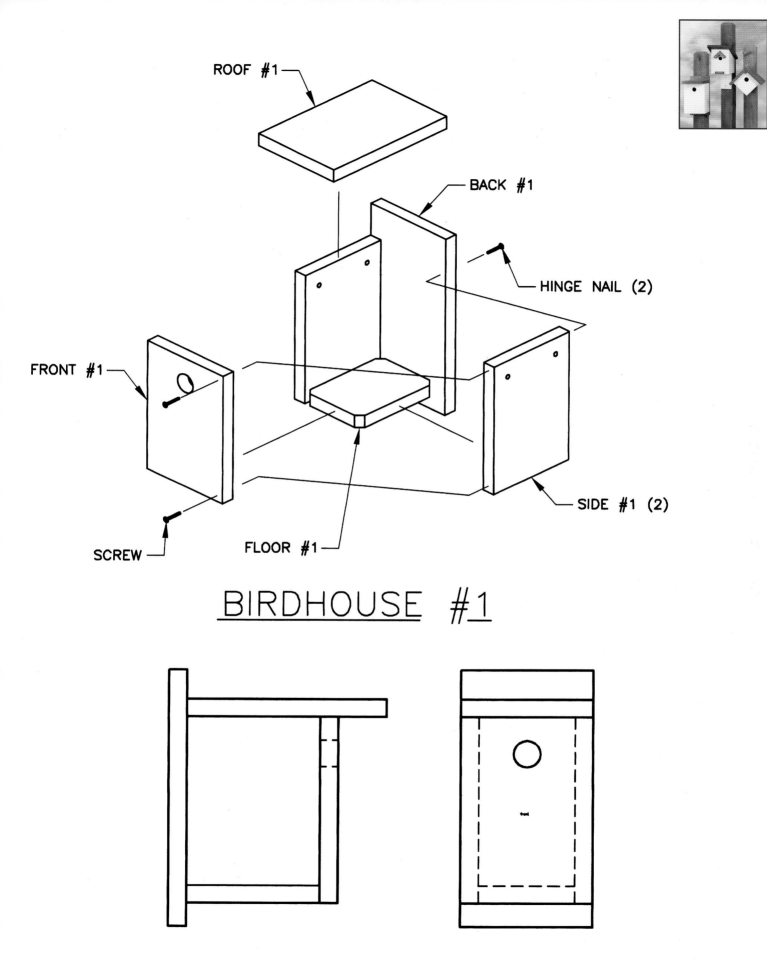

ROOF #1

BACK #1

HINGE NAIL (2)

FRONT #1

SIDE #1 (2)

SCREW

FLOOR #1

BIRDHOUSE #1

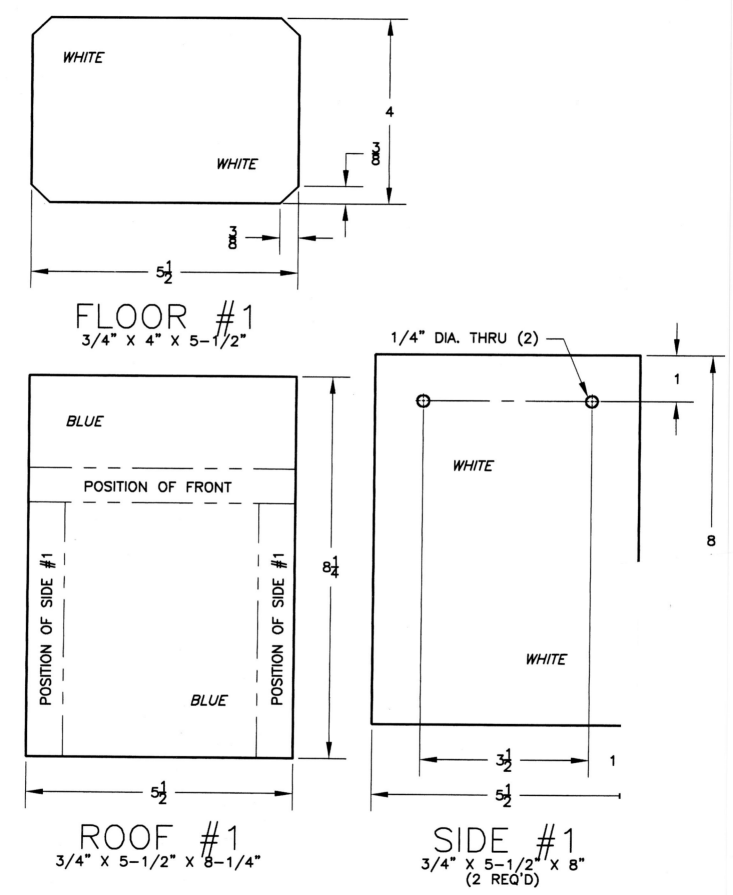

WHITE

WHITE

4

3/8

3/8

5 1/2

FLOOR #1
3/4" X 4" X 5-1/2"

BLUE

POSITION OF FRONT

POSITION OF SIDE #1

POSITION OF SIDE #1

BLUE

8 1/4

5 1/2

ROOF #1
3/4" X 5-1/2" X 8-1/4"

1/4" DIA. THRU (2)

1

WHITE

WHITE

8

3 1/2

1

5 1/2

SIDE #1
3/4" X 5-1/2" X 8"
(2 REQ'D)

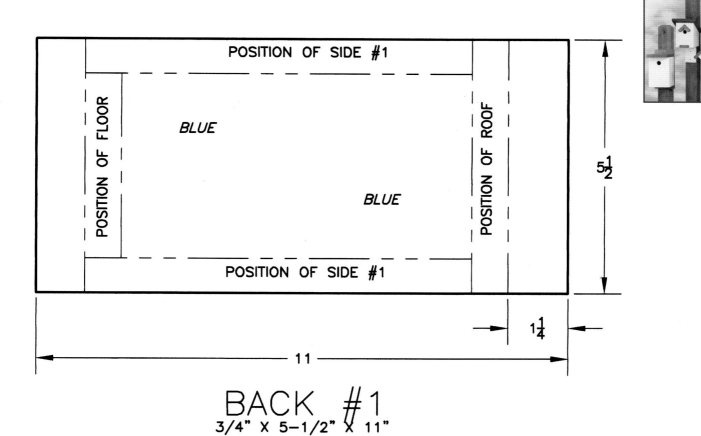

POSITION OF SIDE #1

POSITION OF FLOOR

BLUE

BLUE

POSITION OF ROOF

POSITION OF SIDE #1

$5\frac{1}{2}$

$1\frac{1}{4}$

11

BACK #1
3/4" X 5-1/2" X 11"

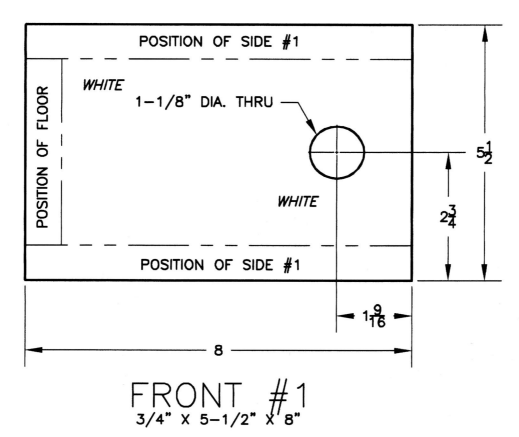

POSITION OF SIDE #1

POSITION OF FLOOR

WHITE

1-1/8" DIA. THRU

WHITE

$5\frac{1}{2}$

$2\frac{3}{4}$

POSITION OF SIDE #1

$1\frac{9}{16}$

8

FRONT #1
3/4" X 5-1/2" X 8"

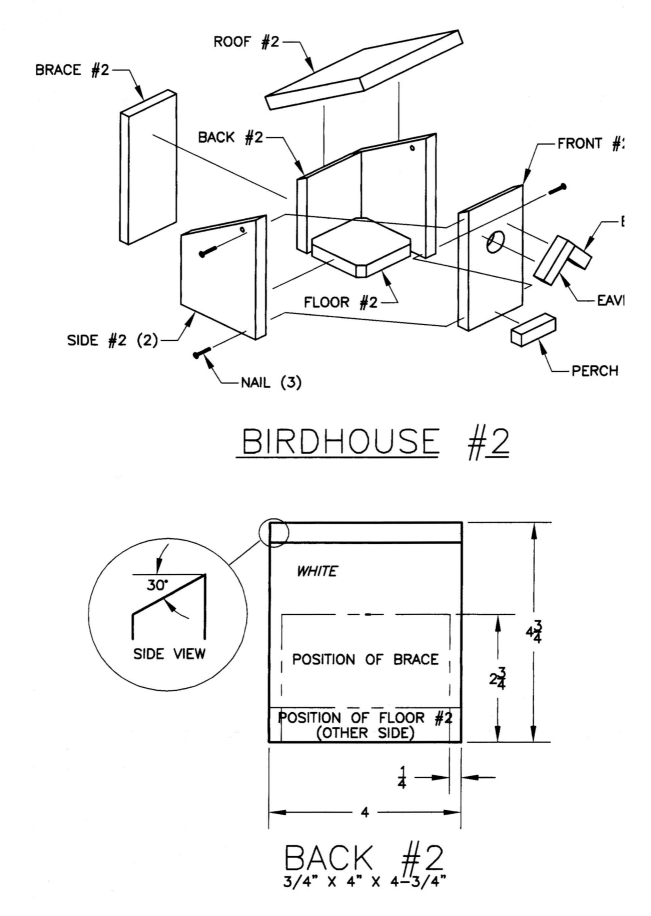

ROOF #2

BRACE #2

BACK #2

FRONT #2

SIDE #2 (2)

FLOOR #2

EAVE

PERCH

NAIL (3)

BIRDHOUSE #2

WHITE

30°

SIDE VIEW

POSITION OF BRACE

POSITION OF FLOOR #2
(OTHER SIDE)

$4\frac{3}{4}$

$2\frac{3}{4}$

$\frac{1}{4}$

4

BACK #2
3/4" X 4" X 4—3/4"

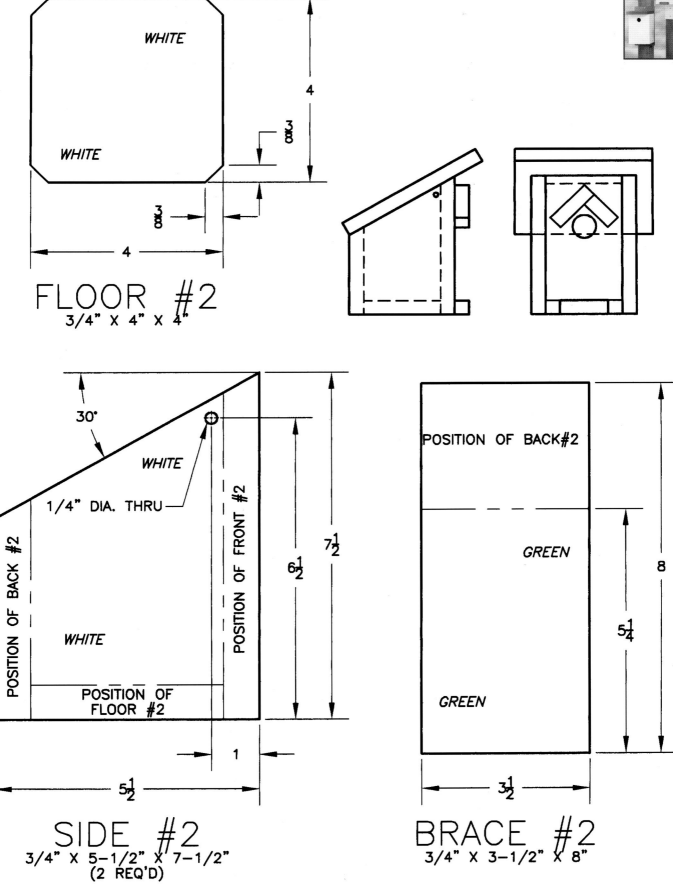

FLOOR #2
3/4" X 4" X 4"

WHITE

WHITE

4

4

3⁄8

3⁄8

SIDE #2
3/4" X 5-1/2" X 7-1/2"
(2 REQ'D)

30°

WHITE

1/4" DIA. THRU

WHITE

POSITION OF BACK #2

POSITION OF FRONT #2

POSITION OF FLOOR #2

7 1⁄2

6 1⁄2

1

5 1⁄2

BRACE #2
3/4" X 3-1/2" X 8"

POSITION OF BACK #2

GREEN

GREEN

8

5 1⁄4

3 1⁄2

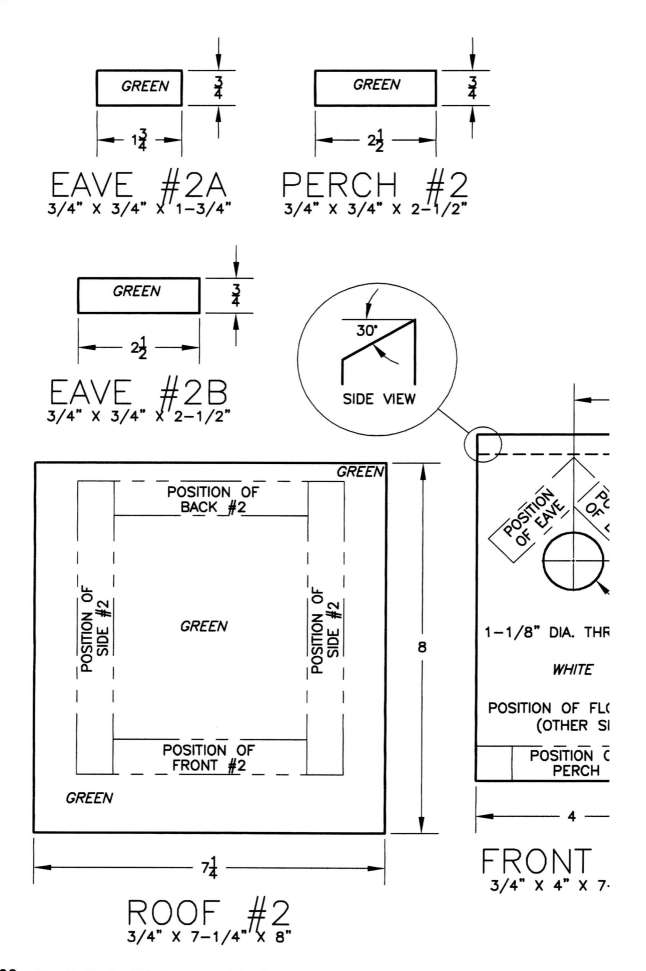

GREEN $\frac{3}{4}$

$1\frac{3}{4}$

EAVE #2A
3/4" X 3/4" X 1–3/4"

GREEN $\frac{3}{4}$

$2\frac{1}{2}$

PERCH #2
3/4" X 3/4" X 2–1/2"

GREEN $\frac{3}{4}$

$2\frac{1}{2}$

EAVE #2B
3/4" X 3/4" X 2–1/2"

30°

SIDE VIEW

GREEN

POSITION OF BACK #2

POSITION OF SIDE #2

GREEN

POSITION OF SIDE #2

8

POSITION OF FRONT #2

GREEN

$7\frac{1}{4}$

ROOF #2
3/4" X 7–1/4" X 8"

POSITION OF EAVE

PO OF

1-1/8" DIA. THR

WHITE

POSITION OF FL(
(OTHER SI

POSITION C
PERCH

4

FRONT
3/4" X 4" X 7·

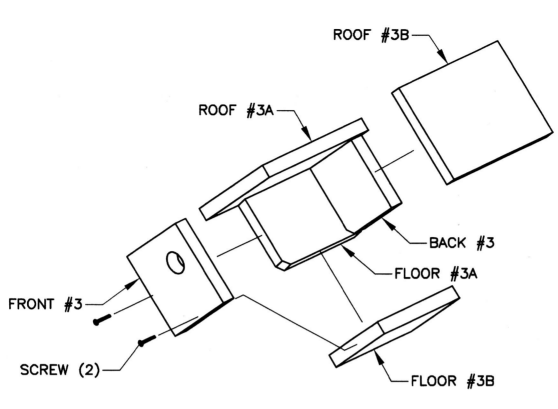

ROOF #3B

ROOF #3A

FRONT #3

SCREW (2)

BACK #3

FLOOR #3A

FLOOR #3B

BIRDHOUSE #3

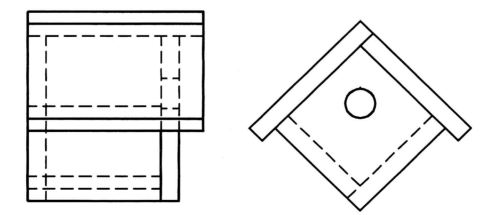

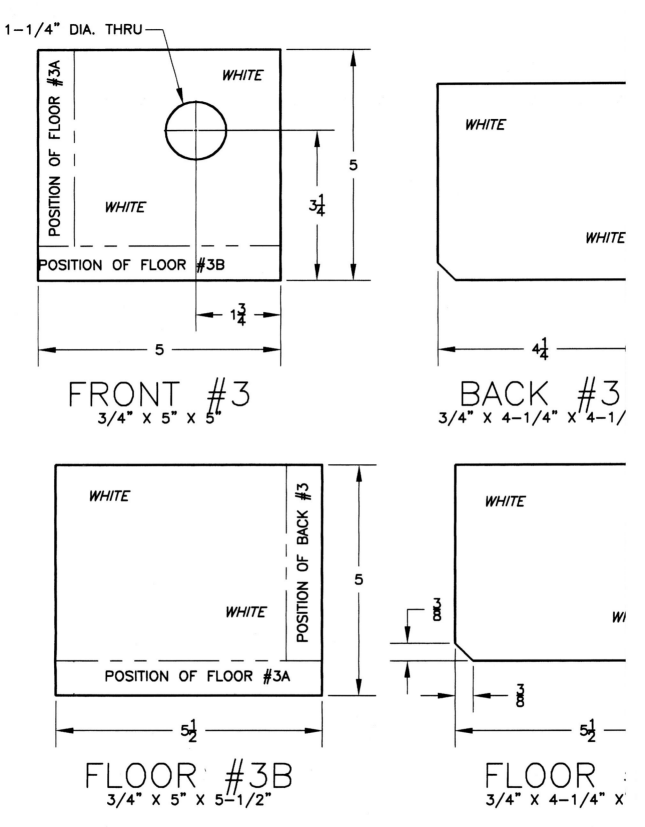

1-1/4" DIA. THRU

POSITION OF FLOOR #3A

WHITE

WHITE

POSITION OF FLOOR #3B

5

$3\frac{1}{4}$

$1\frac{3}{4}$

5

FRONT #3
3/4" X 5" X 5"

WHITE

WHITE

$4\frac{1}{4}$

BACK #3
3/4" X 4-1/4" X 4-1/

WHITE

WHITE

POSITION OF BACK #3

POSITION OF FLOOR #3A

5

$5\frac{1}{2}$

FLOOR #3B
3/4" X 5" X 5-1/2"

WHITE

WI

$5\frac{1}{2}$

FLOOR
3/4" X 4-1/4" X

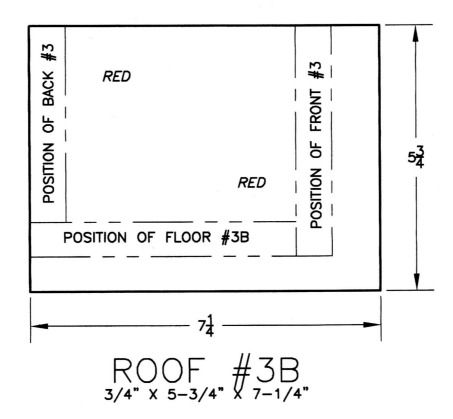

POSITION OF BACK #3

RED

RED

POSITION OF FRONT #3

POSITION OF FLOOR #3B

$5\frac{3}{4}$

$7\frac{1}{4}$

ROOF #3B
3/4" X 5-3/4" X 7-1/4"

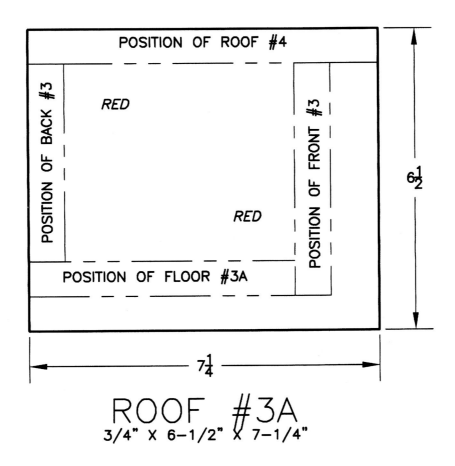

POSITION OF ROOF #4

POSITION OF BACK #3

RED

RED

POSITION OF FRONT #3

POSITION OF FLOOR #3A

$6\frac{1}{2}$

$7\frac{1}{4}$

ROOF #3A
3/4" X 6-1/2" X 7-1/4"

Tylorville Tudor Apartments Birdhouse

Tudor is a style of architecture that became popular in England around the sixteenth century. Tudor was actually the ruling Family of England from 1485–1603, descended from Owen Tudor, a Welsh nobleman who married the widow of Henry V. Today, Tudor architecture is characterized by rounded arches, shallow moldings and extensive paneling. This birdhouse design has only a mild Tudor influence: the vertical slats.

Size-wise, this house is large enough to accommodate larger birds, such as owls and woodpeckers. Because of its size, it should be mounted on a sturdy pole.

PLAN OF PROCEDURE

This project is made from ½" exterior plywood and ¾" stock. To begin, lay out and cut all pieces to size according to the dimensions given in the Bill of Materials. For simplicity, no bevels are required on any of the plywood pieces. One Side is hinged at the top and pivots on ¼" Dowels or Wood Screws so it can be opened for cleaning. This Side is secured with a Wood Screw at the bottom.

Cedar Shakes are optional. Decorative plastic Birdhouse Windows and Doors are attached to the Front and the Back of the house with ⅜" brass Escutcheon Pins.

The Trim strips, the Chimney, the Front Steps and the Door Awning are cut from solid stock. Redwood, cedar or pine can be used. Short lengths of ¼" Dowel rod are used for the decoration on top of the Chimney and can be used for the pivot Hinges for the Side.

FINAL ASSEMBLY

Paint: Paint the project as desired. Acr┊ and gloss or semi-gloss exterior acrylic recommended. I used exterior stain an┊ brick red paint for this project.

Step 1: Attach the Front, the Back, one Si┊ pieces together. The remaining Side i┊ open for cleaning and should not be glu┊

Step 2: Fit the remaining Side (with the ┊ it slips into place between the Front and ¼" x 1¼" Dowels through the ¹⁷⁄₆₄" h┊ and the Back and into the ¼" holes i┊ Dowels act as Hinges. The Side shoul┊ as there must be some room for swell┊ piece. If the piece fits too tightly, it will for cleaning.

Step 3: Cut the Roof to size and attach. Gl┊ and the Smokestacks in place.

Step 4: Glue the Trim and the Front Step┊

Step 5: The illustration shows suggested Windows and the Door. Mark the l┊ Windows and the Door and paint the a┊ black. Attach the Trim.

Step 6: The Door and the Windows ar┊ ⅜" x #18 Escutcheon Pins. Cedar attached with hot melt glue, epoxy or┊ Be sure the swinging Side remains free t┊ Drill a hole through the Front and in┊ Side for a Wood Screw to secure the Si┊

 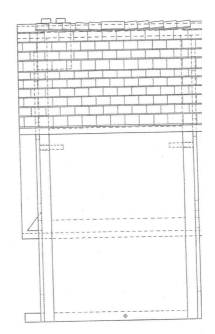

TYLORVILLE TUDOR APARTMENTS BIRDHOUSE: BILL OF MATERIALS

Quantity	Part #	Description	Size of Material
2	#1	Front/Back	½" x 14⅞" x 15½"
1	#2	Side	½" x 7" x 5½"
1	#3	Side	½" x 7" x 10½"
1	#4	Floor	½" x 7" x 13⅞"
1	#5	Roof	½" x 10" x 8"
1	#6	Roof	½" x 10" x 15½"
1	#7	Chimney	1" x 1¾" x 2½"
2	#8	Smokestack	¼" dia. x ¼"
10	#9	Trim	³⁄₁₆" x ⅜" x (see drawin
2	#10	Hinge (Dowels)	¼" dia. x 1¼"
1	#11	Front Steps	½" x 1" x 3½"
1	#12	Door Awning	¾" x 1" x 2-½"
1	#13	Wood Screw	1¼" x #6
10	*#14	Birdhouse Window (#8607)	1½" x 3½"
1	*#15	Birdhouse Door (#8606)	2" x 4½"
Misc.	*#16	Cedar Shakes (#7688)	¹⁄₁₆" x ¾" x 1¼"
Misc.	*#17	Escutcheon Pin (#388)	⅜" x #18

*Available from Meisel Har

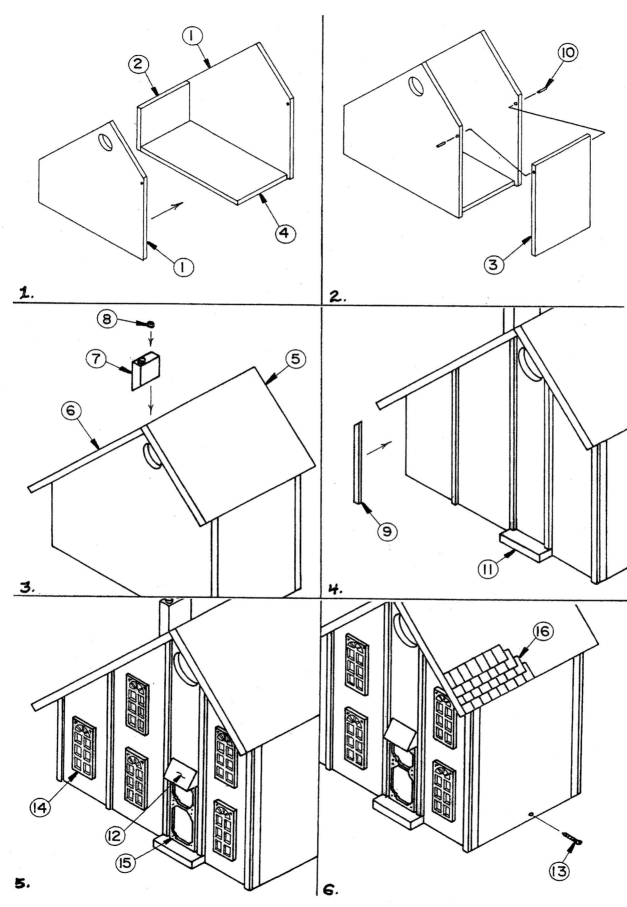

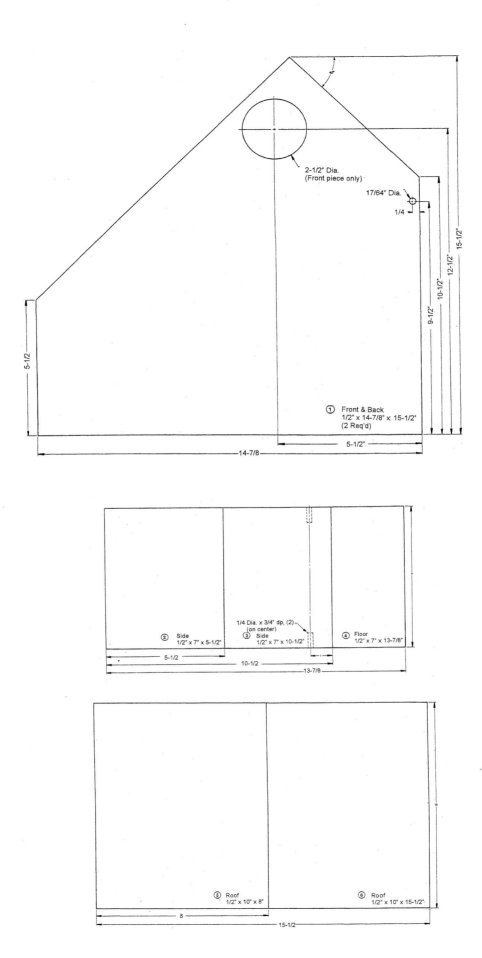

2-1/2" Dia.
(Front piece only)

17/64" Dia.

1/4

① Front & Back
1/2" x 14-7/8" x 15-1/2"
(2 Req'd)

② Side
1/2" x 7" x 5-1/2"

③ Side
1/2" x 7" x 10-1/2"

1/4 Dia. x 3/4" dp, (2)
(on center)

④ Floor
1/2" x 7" x 13-7/8"

⑤ Roof
1/2" x 10" x 8"

⑥ Roof
1/2" x 10" x 15-1/2"

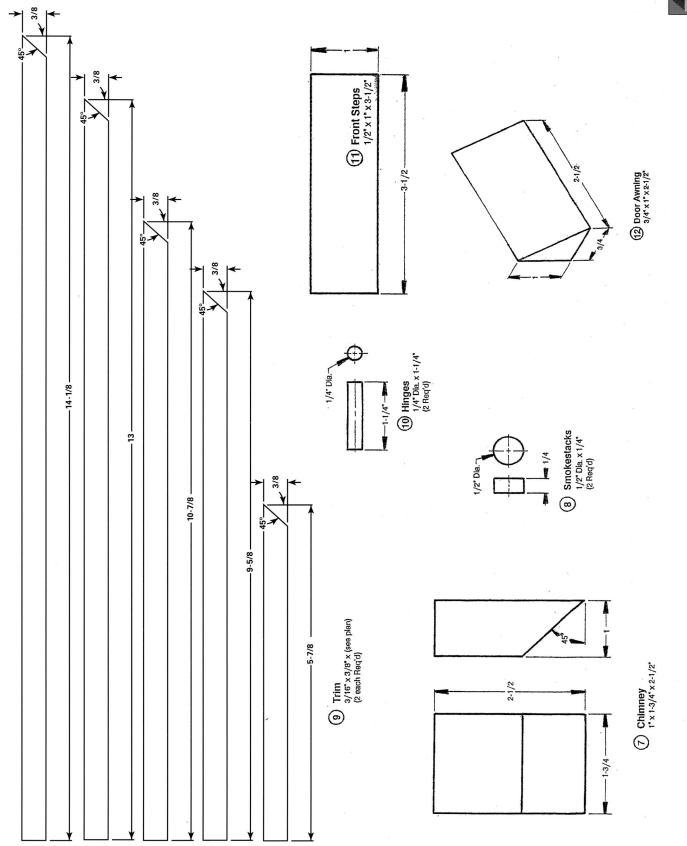

3/8
45°

3/8
45°

3/8
45°

3/8
45°

3/8
45°

14-1/8

13

10-7/8

9-5/8

5-7/8

⑨ Trim
3/16" x 3/8" x (see plan)
(2 each Req'd)

⑪ Front Steps
1/2" x 1" x 3-1/2"

3-1/2

⑩ Hinges
1/4" Dia. x 1-1/4"
(2 Req'd)

1/4" Dia.

1-1/4"

⑫ Door Awning
3/4" x 1" x 2-1/2"

2-1/2"

3/4

⑧ Smokestacks
1/2" Dia. x 1/4"
(2 Req'd)

1/2" Dia.

1/4

⑦ Chimney
1" x 1-3/4" x 2-1/2"

45°

1

2-1/2

1-3/4

How-To Book of Birdhouses and Feeders • 109

The White House Birdhouse

The White House is the executive mansion and official residence of the President of the United States. It was built from the design of James Hoban in what was described, at that time, as a simple and dignified style. This birdhouse was designed after the front, or north side, of the house, facing Pennsylvania Avenue.

The birdhouse features the pillared portico, which shelters the entrance and is recognizable by the tall columns. It is a duplex in that it will house two families of birds. There is a partition in the center and an entrance hole on each side. The partition can be omitted if you want one large cavity. In that case, omit one entrance hole.

WHITE HOUSE BIRDHOUSE: PLAN OF PROCEDURE

This project is made from ½" exterior plywood and ¾" stock. Lay out and cut all pieces to size according to the dimensions given in the Bill of Materials. The Front, the Back, the Partition, the Roof and the Steps are not drawn since they are simple rectangular-shaped pieces. Both Top and Front View Drawings are provided for the Facade pieces.

Drill all holes as required. The Final Ass[...] to the illustrations on the following page[...] can be cut from ⅛" exterior plywood an[...] Alternately, the Window pieces can be om[...] Windows painted directly on the Front pi[...]

FINAL ASSEMBLY

Step 1: Attach the Front, the Back, th[...] Partition as shown.

Step 2: Glue the Columns in the ½" diam[...] Floor. Glue the Façade to the Colum[...] fashion. Attach the Steps to the front c[...]

Step 3: Attach the Floor to the sub-assem[...] Attach the First Floor and the Second F[...] the Front as shown.

Step 4: Attach the Roof with the 1¼" x ≠[...] An eagle can be painted on the Front[...] attached for added charm.

Paint: Paint the project as desired. Acr[...] and gloss or semi-gloss exterior acr[...] are recommended. I used winter white[...] this project.

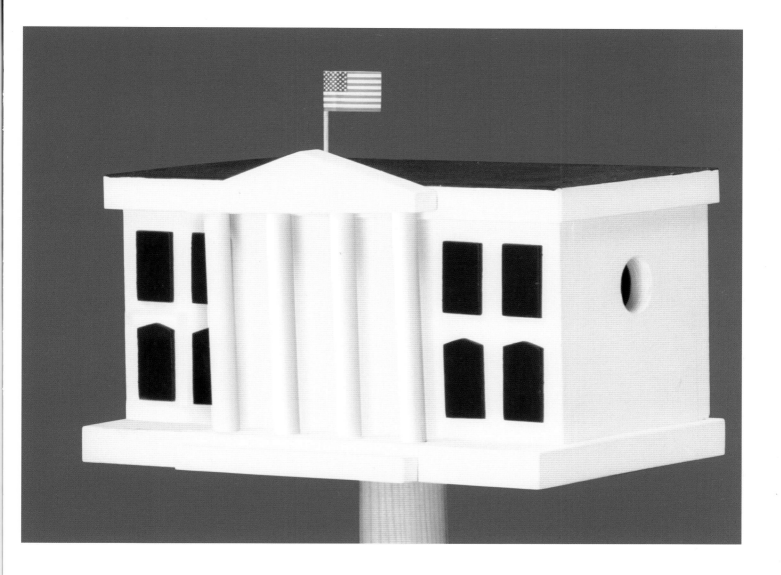

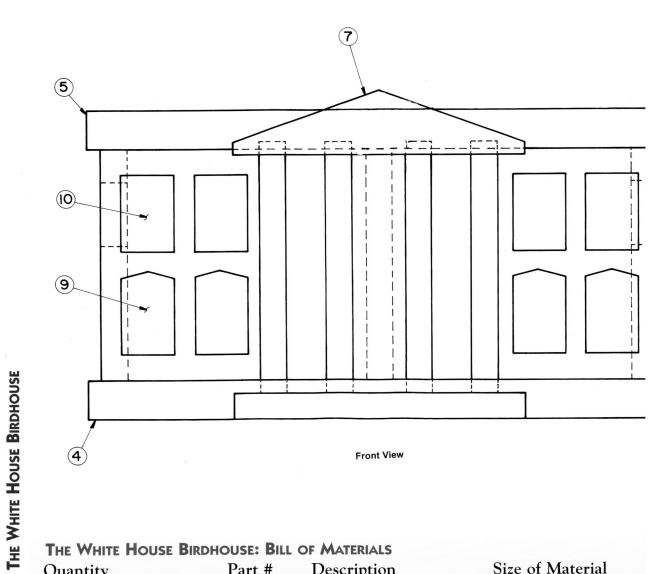

Front View

THE WHITE HOUSE BIRDHOUSE: BILL OF MATERIALS

Quantity	Part #	Description	Size of Material
2	#1	Front/Back	$\frac{1}{2}$" x $4\frac{1}{2}$" x $10\frac{1}{2}$"
2	#2	Side	$\frac{1}{2}$" x $4\frac{1}{2}$" x $4\frac{3}{4}$"
1	#3	Partition	$\frac{1}{2}$" x $4\frac{1}{2}$" x $4\frac{3}{4}$"
1	#4	Floor	$\frac{3}{4}$" x 7" x 11"
1	#5	Roof	$\frac{3}{4}$" x $6\frac{1}{8}$" x 11"
4	#6	Column (Dowels)	$\frac{1}{2}$" dia. x $4\frac{7}{8}$"
1	#7	Facade	$\frac{3}{4}$" x $1\frac{1}{4}$" x $5\frac{1}{2}$"
1	#8	Steps	$\frac{1}{2}$" x $\frac{1}{2}$" x $5\frac{1}{2}$"
4	#9	First Floor Window	$\frac{1}{8}$" x 1" x $1\frac{5}{8}$"
4	#10	Second Floor Window	$\frac{1}{8}$" x 1" x $1\frac{1}{2}$"
4	#11	Wood Screw	$1\frac{1}{4}$" x #8

1.

2.

3.

4.

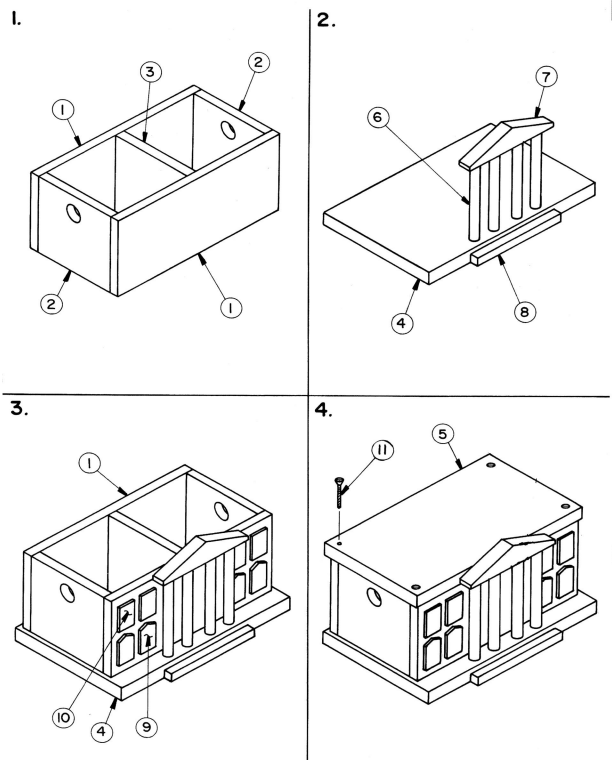

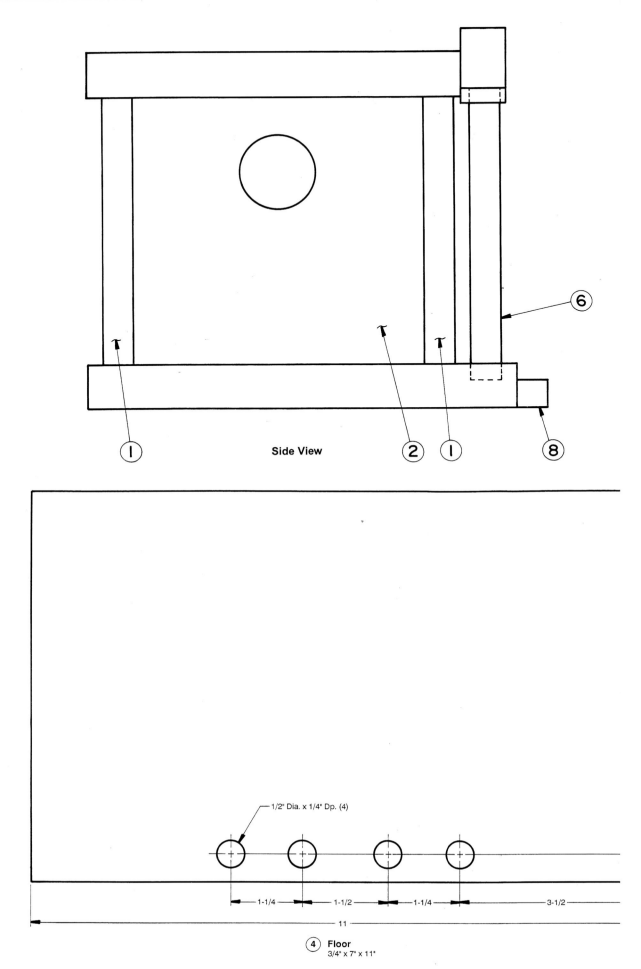

Side View

1/2" Dia. x 1/4" Dp. (4)

1-1/4   1-1/2   1-1/4   3-1/2

11

④ Floor
3/4" x 7" x 11"

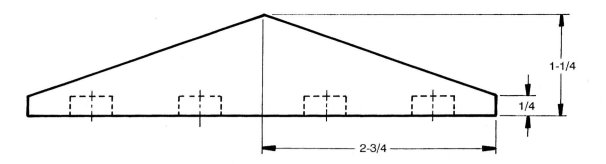

1-1/4

1/4

2-3/4

1/2" Dia. x 1/4" Dp. (4)

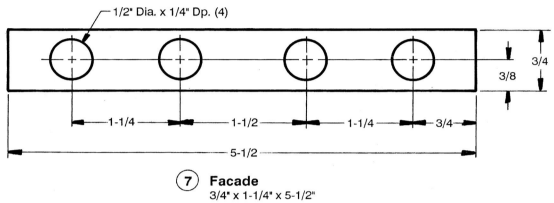

3/4

3/8

1-1/4   1-1/2   1-1/4   3/4

5-1/2

(7) **Facade**
3/4" x 1-1/4" x 5-1/2"

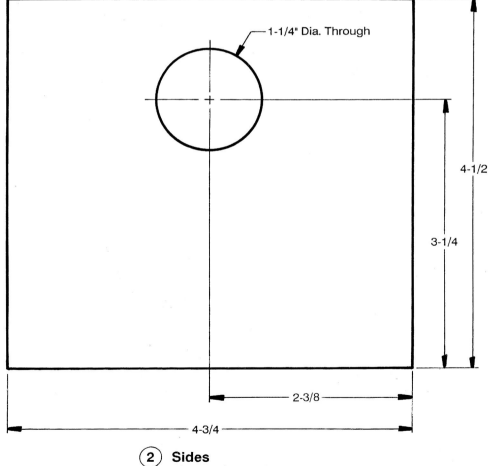

1-1/4" Dia. Through

4-1/2

3-1/4

2-3/8

4-3/4

(2) **Sides**
1/2" x 4-1/2" x 4-3/4"
(2 REQ'D)

Wren Row Birdhouse

This project is based on the row house, a group of identical houses joined along sides by common walls. Row houses are similar to town houses, except that they often appear to be very narrow in width. This style of house is especially popular in many Eastern cities.

This birdhouse has design elements that reflect two of the features often associated with this type of housing. The house itself is tall and narrow and it makes generous use of high and narrow windows. It will accommodate a variety of birds, has a unique look and is easy to build. Although pictured with clapboard siding, this project would, instead, be an excellent candidate for a simple paint finish in the color of red or brown or brick.

WREN ROW BIRDHOUSE: PLAN OF PROCEDURE

Before beginning construction, decide what type of bird you wish to attract. The house can be built as one large cavity by leaving off one of the floor pieces. If you add both floor pieces, you will have two small cavities (two floors). If you would like the birds to use the upper floor as a cavity, cut away part of the upper rear window as shown on the drawing (see the dotted line) and drill the entrance holes.

All drawings have been reduced in size. Use layout tools to transfer the drawings to the plywood.

The notes on the drawing of the Front and Back piece indicate where to drill the Entrance holes. If you are making a simple one-cavity house, drill only one hole in the first Floor on the Front piece. If you are building a two-cavity house, drill the second hole in the second Floor on the Back of the house. Note that the 1/4" holes in the Side drawing are for the purpose of making wood dowel hinges. These 1/4" holes are drilled in one Side piece only. Drill a screw clearance hole at the bottom of the Hinged Side piece to hold it closed. (See the drawing of the Side view of the assembled house.)

Drawings are not provided for the Trim pieces. They are simple rectangular-shap them to the size given in the Bill of Materi

To begin, layout and cut all pieces to size all holes as required. Finish-sand all parts steps refer to the step-by-step illustrations. I instructions are for a two-room birdhouse.

Clapboard siding is optional. It is avai house suppliers. Although it gives the bird look, I do not necessarily recommend using to glue it securely, and it can have a tendenc after several rains.

Step 1: Glue the Front and Back, one Sid pieces together.

Step 2: Sand the Side piece with the 1/4" slips into place between the Front and I 1/4" x 1 1/4" wood dowels through the 1/4 Front and Back and into the 1/4" holes in Side should fit snug yet swing open for cl

Step 3: Glue the Roof pieces to the Front the Chimney to the Roof and the Sm Chimney.

Step 4: Glue the Trim and Steps in place. glue the swinging Side shut.

Step 5: Cut the rear upstairs Window entrance hole. Paint the area behind the Paint the Trim before painting the roof (shingles).

FINAL ASSEMBLY

Paint or shingle the Roof. Drill a 7/64" install the 1 5/8" x #6 screw to secure th painting the project. Nail the windows and with Escutcheon Pins.

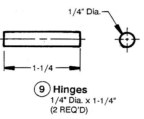

(7) **Smokestacks**
1/2" Dia. x 1/4"
(2 REQ'D)

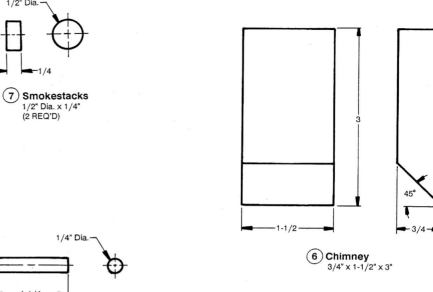

(6) **Chimney**
3/4" x 1-1/2" x 3"

(9) **Hinges**
1/4" Dia. x 1-1/4"
(2 REQ'D)

WREN ROW BIRDHOUSE: BILL OF MATERIALS

Quantity	Part #	Description	Size of Material
1	#1	Front and Back	¾" x 5½" x 14¼"
2	#2	Sides	¾" x 6½" x 11½"
2	#3	Floor	¾" x 4½" x 6¼" (not s
1	#4	Roof	¾" x 4¾" x 9½" (not s
1	#5	Roof	¾" x 5¼" x 9½" (not s
1	#6	Chimney	¾" x 1½" x 3"
2	#7	Smokestack	½" dia x ¼"
1	#8	Steps	¾" x 1" x 4"
2	#9	Hinges	¼" dia x 1¼"
4	#10	Trim	3/16" x 5/8" x 11⅜" (not
11	#11	*Windows (#8607)	1½" x 3½"
1	#12	*Door (#8606)	2" x 4½"
1	#13	*Trim Head Fin. Screw (#6278)	1⅝" x #6
misc.	#14	*Cedar Shakes (#7688)	
misc.	#15	Doll House Siding (optional)	
misc.	#16	*Escutcheon Pins (#388)	⅜" x #18

*Available from Meisel Hardw

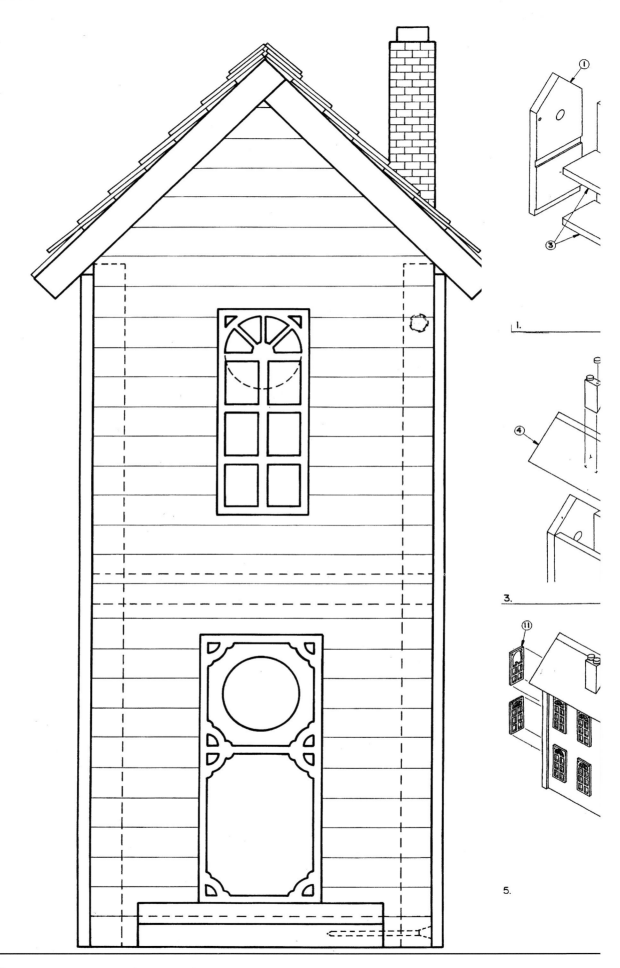

1.

3.

5.

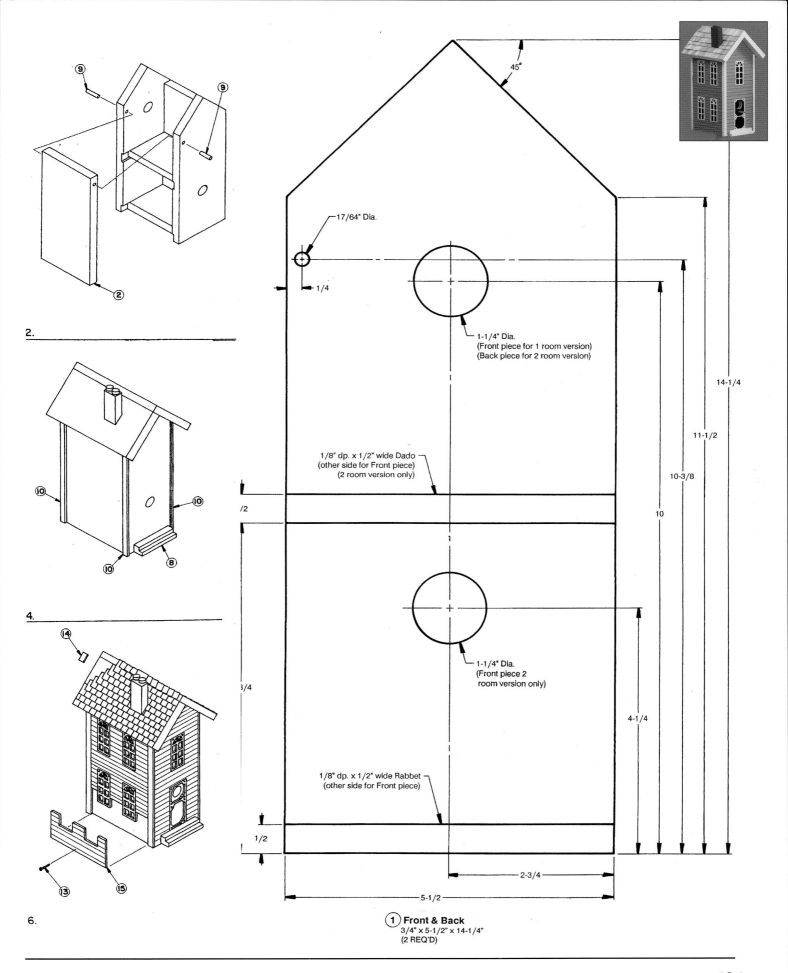

2.

4.

6.

17/64" Dia.

1/4

1-1/4" Dia.
(Front piece for 1 room version)
(Back piece for 2 room version)

45°

14-1/4

11-1/2

10-3/8

10

1/8" dp. x 1/2" wide Dado
(other side for Front piece)
(2 room version only)

1/2

1-1/4" Dia.
(Front piece 2
room version only)

4-1/4

3/4

1/8" dp. x 1/2" wide Rabbet
(other side for Front piece)

1/2

2-3/4

5-1/2

① Front & Back
3/4" x 5-1/2" x 14-1/4"
(2 REQ'D)

1/4" Dia. x 3/4" dp. O.C. (2)
(one piece only)

11-1/2

10-3/8

6-1/2

(2) Sides
3/4" x 6-1/2" x 11-1/2"
(2 REQ'D)

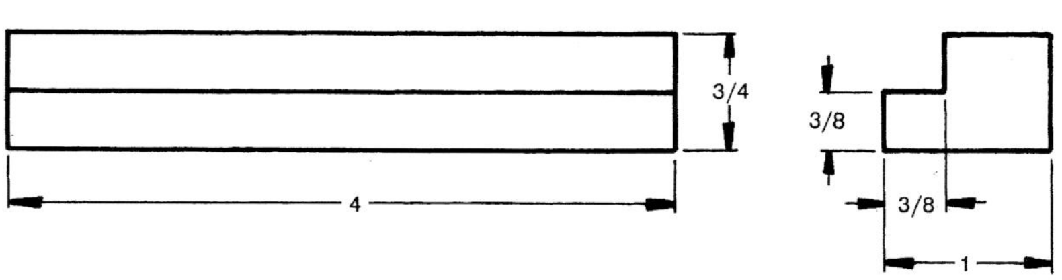

3/4

4

3/8

3/8

1

(8) Steps
3/4" x 1" x 4"

Part Three
Birdfeeders

Adirondack Birdfeeder

This little birdfeeder is a tiny Adirondack lawn chair. It is truly a workable birdfeeder. I put it in the yard and sure enough, the birds came; although, I think they liked it better after I took the painted wood bird off.

Because this birdfeeder is so small, this project should probably be looked at as a novelty. It is great to set in the yard for fun. Or perhaps you'll want to build several and use them as drink holders. Used in this way, they become a type of "humanfeeder."

One unique thing about the mounting method is that it uses a ⅜" diameter by 36"-long fiberglass rod. These rods are very sturdy and easy to poke into the ground and, more importantly, pull out of the ground when it is time to mow the lawn.

PLAN OF PROCEDURE

This project can be made from two ⅜" x 1' x 1' pieces of exterior plywood. The only exception is the Back, which is ¾" thick and can be made from a scrap piece of pine. The reason it is thicker is because a ⅜" hole needs to be drilled in this piece to hold the ⅜" fiberglass rod used for mounting.

The Arm Brace, the Back Brace, the Front and the Side pieces are simple rectangular-shaped pieces of plywood. Cut them to the length and width given in the Bill of Materials. A standard window screen is stapled to the bottom to hold the birdseed.

Assembly is done with water-resistant glue and wire brads. Pre-drill the holes for the wire brads to avoid bending them when nailing them into the birch plywood. The pattern for the bird is provided in the Sleeping Cat Birdfeeder chapter.

Chair Back #1, #2, and #3: Lay out and cut to size from ⅜" stock. (Two Pieces Required for Chair Back #1 and #2)

Rear Leg: Lay out and cut to size f (Two Pieces Required)

Front Leg: Lay out and cut to size : (Two Pieces Required)

Arm: Lay out and cut to size from ⅜" st Required)

Arm Support: Lay out and cut to size Transfer the pattern and cut out. (Two l

Arm Brace: Lay out and cut to size from ⅜

Back Brace: Lay out and cut to size from

Front: Lay out and cut to size from ⅜" st

Back: Lay out and cut to size from ¾" 15-degree bevel.

Side: Lay out and cut to size from ⅜" st Required)

Wire Screen: Lay out and cut to the size of Materials.

FINAL ASSEMBLY

Step 1: Assemble the Front, the Side and Attach the Front Legs and the Rear I pieces. Attach the Arms and Arm Supp Legs. Attach the Arm Brace to the A Back Brace to Chair Back #1, #2 and # Attach the Chair Back to the Back Bra Brace.

Step 2: Drill a ⅜" diameter x ⅝" deep ho of the Back and the Chair Back #3 Fiberglass Rod. Epoxy glue may be used Rod if desired. Attach the Wire Screen the Front, Side and Back pieces.

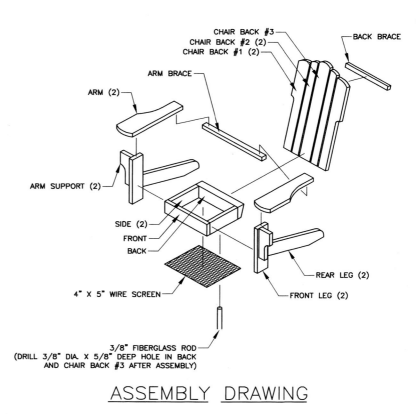

CHAIR BACK #3
CHAIR BACK #2 (2)
CHAIR BACK #1 (2)
BACK BRACE
ARM BRACE
ARM (2)
ARM SUPPORT (2)
SIDE (2)
FRONT
BACK
4" X 5" WIRE SCREEN
REAR LEG (2)
FRONT LEG (2)
3/8" FIBERGLASS ROD
(DRILL 3/8" DIA. X 5/8" DEEP HOLE IN BACK
AND CHAIR BACK #3 AFTER ASSEMBLY)

ASSEMBLY DRAWING

ADIRONDACK BIRDFEEDER: BILL OF MATERIALS

Quantity	Description	Size of Material
2	Chair Back #1	$\frac{3}{8}$" x $1\frac{1}{4}$" x $8\frac{3}{4}$"
2	Chair Back #2	$\frac{3}{8}$" x $\frac{3}{4}$" x $9\frac{1}{8}$"
1	Chair Back #3	$\frac{3}{8}$" x $1\frac{1}{4}$" x $9\frac{1}{2}$"
2	Rear Leg	$\frac{3}{8}$" x $1\frac{1}{4}$" x $7\frac{3}{32}$"
2	Front Leg	$\frac{3}{8}$" x $1\frac{1}{4}$" x $4\frac{3}{4}$"
2	Arm	$\frac{3}{8}$" x $1\frac{7}{8}$" x $6\frac{1}{4}$"
2	Arm Support	$\frac{3}{8}$" x $1\frac{1}{4}$" x $3\frac{1}{8}$"
1	Arm Brace	$\frac{3}{8}$" x $\frac{1}{2}$" x 7"
1	Back Brace	$\frac{3}{8}$" x $\frac{3}{8}$" x 5"
1	Front	$\frac{3}{8}$" x $1\frac{1}{4}$" x 5"
1	Back	$\frac{3}{4}$" x $1\frac{1}{4}$" x 5"
2	Side	$\frac{3}{8}$" x $1\frac{1}{4}$" x $3\frac{5}{16}$"
1	Wire Screen	4" x 5"
1	*Fiberglass Rod (#8640)	$\frac{3}{8}$" dia. x 36"

*Available from Meisel Har

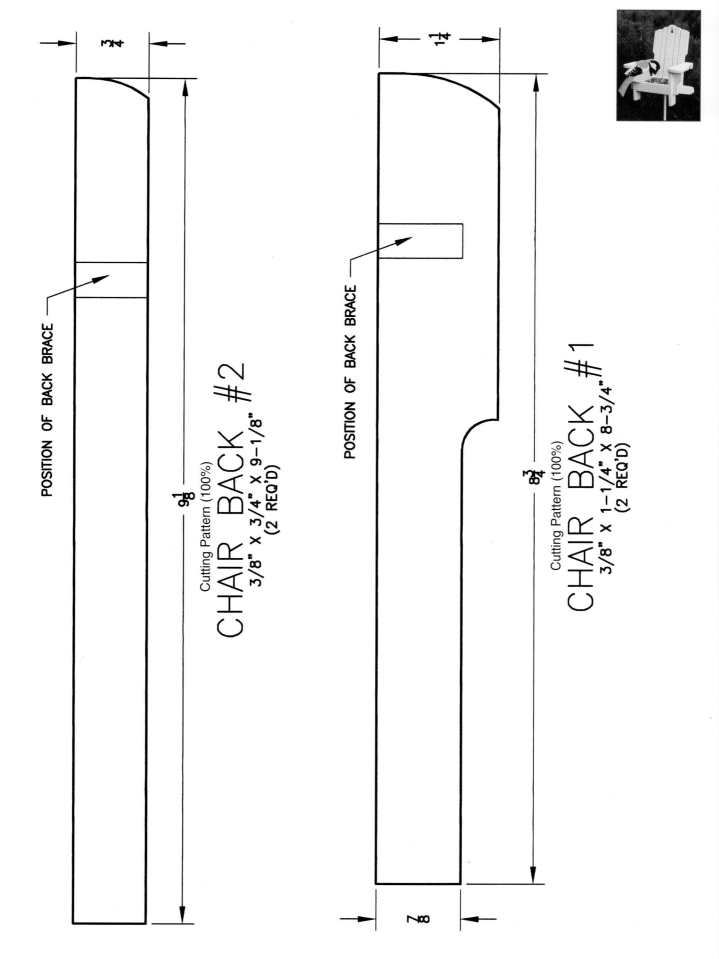

POSITION OF BACK BRACE

$\frac{3}{4}$

$9\frac{1}{8}$

Cutting Pattern (100%)

CHAIR BACK #2
3/8" x 3/4" x 9–1/8"
(2 REQ'D)

POSITION OF BACK BRACE

$1\frac{1}{4}$

$8\frac{3}{4}$

$\frac{7}{8}$

Cutting Pattern (100%)

CHAIR BACK #1
3/8" x 1–1/4" x 8–3/4"
(2 REQ'D)

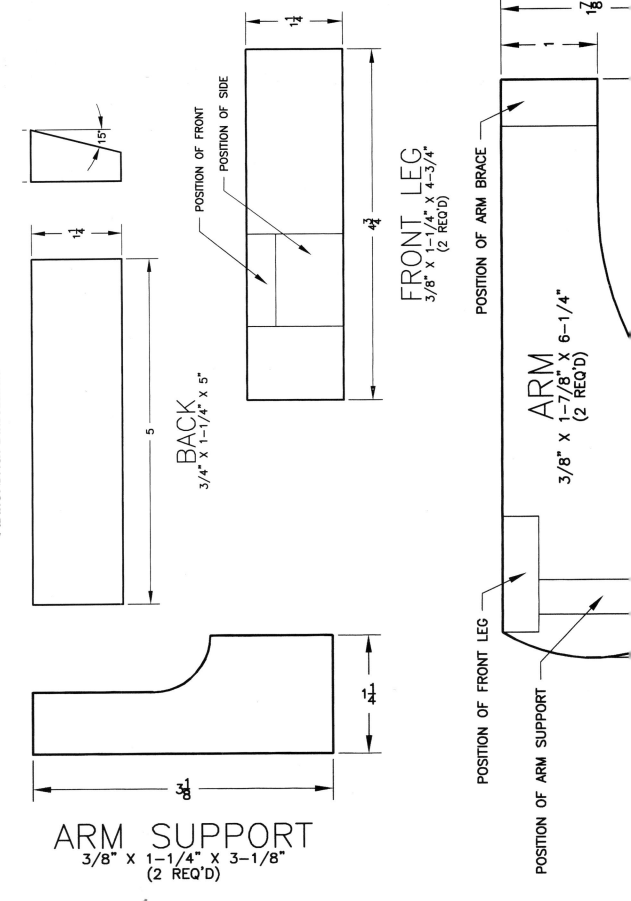

ADIRONDACK BIRDFEEDER

BACK
3/4" X 1-1/4" x 5"

FRONT LEG
3/8" X 1-1/4" X 4-3/4"
(2 REQ'D)

POSITION OF FRONT

POSITION OF SIDE

ARM
3/8" X 1-7/8" X 6-1/4"
(2 REQ'D)

POSITION OF ARM BRACE

POSITION OF FRONT LEG

POSITION OF ARM SUPPORT

ARM SUPPORT
3/8" X 1-1/4" X 3-1/8"
(2 REQ'D)

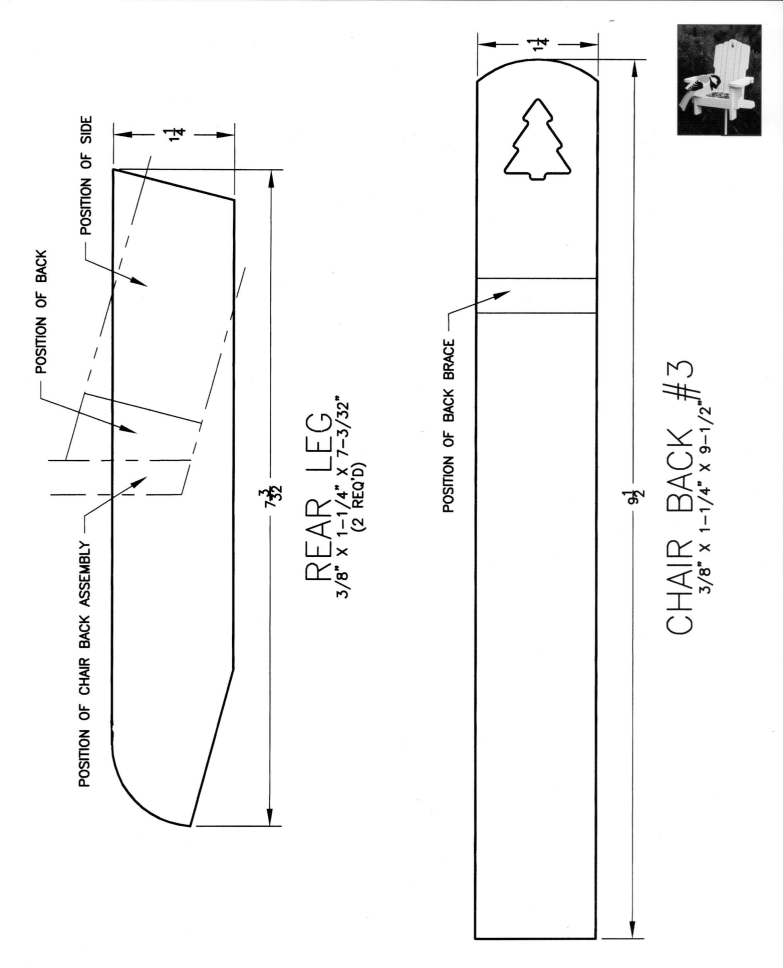

REAR LEG
3/8" X 1–1/4" X 7–3/32"
(2 REQ'D)

POSITION OF BACK

POSITION OF SIDE

POSITION OF CHAIR BACK ASSEMBLY

$7\frac{3}{32}$

$1\frac{1}{4}$

CHAIR BACK #3
3/8" X 1–1/4" X 9–1/2"

POSITION OF BACK BRACE

$9\frac{1}{2}$

$1\frac{1}{4}$

Cardinal Birdfeeder

The male American cardinal is one of the most colorful birds you're likely to have visit your feeder. Cardinals can be found in most regions of the continental United States.

This project looks quite pleasing when made from redwood as pictured. The cardinal is cut from solid ¾" stock. If you can't find a board wide enough, you will have to edge-glue two or more narrow pieces together. Be sure to use water-resistant glue.

PLAN OF PROCEDURE

The Cardinal: Use a scroll saw to cut the Cardinal from ¾" solid stock. All lines are cut lines. For each of the inside cuts, drill a small hole, thread the scroll saw blade through, and then cut the detail. The cut lines should be wider than the width of a scroll saw blade; therefore it is necessary to make two cuts very close to each other to create the desired width. Cut these detail lines about ¹⁄₁₆" wide.

Note: The Front, Back and Side Pieces as well as the Post

are identical to those used in the Flutter[
page 140.

Cardinal: Transfer the pattern onto ¾"
cut out.

Front and Back, Side, Post, Wire Scre
pieces as shown in the Flutterby Birdfee[
page 140.)

Sanding: Finish sanding all parts. I use
followed by a coat exterior polyurethane f[

FINAL ASSEMBLY

Assemble the Front and Back piece an[
shown in the illustration. Attach the Card[
of this mitered assembly. Attach the tra[
the Post.

Apply wood finish according to the
instructions. Last attach the Wire Screen
the mitered box with a staple gun. Insert
ground to display the finished project.

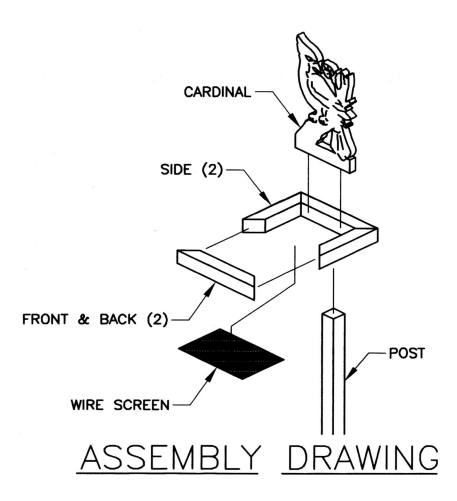

CARDINAL

SIDE (2)

FRONT & BACK (2)

POST

WIRE SCREEN

ASSEMBLY DRAWING

CARDINAL BIRDFEEDER: BILL OF MATERIALS

Quantity	Description	Size of Material
1	Cardinal	¾" x 7¼" x 12⅞"
2	Front & Back	1½" x 1½" x 10¼"
2	Side	1½" x 1½" x 7¾"
1	Post	1½" x 1½" x 60"
1	Wire Screen	5¼" x 8¼"

*Available from Meisel Hardware Spe

CARDINAL
3/4" X 7-1/4" X 12-7/8"
(Enlarge 200%)

$1\frac{1}{2}$

$7\frac{1}{4}$

Covered Bridge Birdfeeder

A number of years ago, a movie came out named The Bridges of Madison County. It starred Meryl Streep and Clint Eastwood. It was a very popular movie.

Madison County is in Iowa. Some of the footage was filmed on location. After the movie came out, the covered bridges became quite a tourist attraction. In fact, after we saw the movie, my wife and I decided to visit Madison County. From our home in Minnesota, it's only about a five-hour ride. For us it was a delightful summer motorcycle trip. Even though the bridges are very old, they are in remarkably good shape. It was just after this trip that I designed the Covered Bridge Birdfeeder.

PLAN OF PROCEDURE

This project can be made from one piece of 1x8 pine. The Roof helps to keep the birdseed dry. Galley Spindles hold the landing perch (the Rail pieces) in a raised position. The Wire Screen is standard window screen.

Rail: Lay out and cut to size from ¾" stock. Drill the ¼" diameter x ¼" deep holes for the Galley Spindles. (Two Pieces Required)

Roof Support: Lay out and cut to size from ¾" stock. (Four Pieces Required)

Support: Lay out and cut to size from ¾" stock. (Two Pieces Required)

Base End: Lay out and cut to size fr⊙ (Two Pieces Required)

Base Side: Lay out and cut to size from ¾" ¼" diameter x ¼" deep holes for the G (Two Pieces Required)

Roof: Lay out and cut to size from ¾" 30-degree bevel. (Two Pieces Required)

Roof Mount: Transfer the pattern onto ¾" out. Drill the 1" diameter hole. (Two Piec

Wire Screen: Lay out and cut to size from stock according to the dimensions given Materials.

FINAL ASSEMBLY

Step 1: Attach the Base Ends to the Base Si⊙ Supports to the bottom of the Base Side should be centered side-to-side and end-to the Galley Spindles and the Rails with the B exterior glue.

Step 2: Attach the Roof Supports to the R⊙ position shown on the full-size drawing of th piece. Attach the Roof Supports to the Ba with the ends of the Rails. Attach the Roo Roof Mounts. Staple the Wire Screen to the Base Assembly. Insert the Screw Eyes in th Roof and hang the project with a rope or a cl

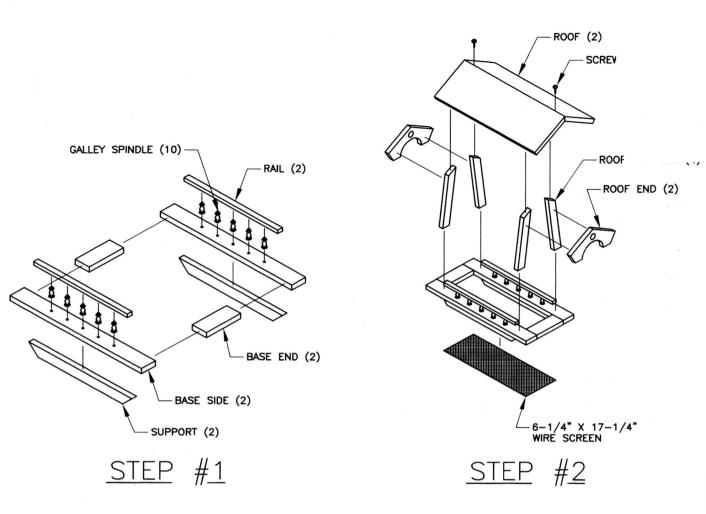

GALLEY SPINDLE (10)

RAIL (2)

BASE END (2)

BASE SIDE (2)

SUPPORT (2)

ROOF (2)

SCREW

ROOF

ROOF END (2)

6-1/4" X 17-1/4" WIRE SCREEN

STEP #1

STEP #2

COVERED BRIDGE BIRDFEEDER: BILL OF MATERIALS

Quantity	Description	Size of Material
2	Rail	½" x ¾" x 15"
4	Roof Support	¾" x 1⅜" x 10⅜"
2	Support	¾" x 1½" x 16½"
2	Base End	¾" x 2¼" x 5½"
2	Base Side	¾" x 2¼" x 21"
2	Roof	¾" x 7¼" x 21"
2	Roof Mount	¾" x 4½" x 9⁵⁄₁₆"
1	Wire Screen	6¼" x 17¼"
10	*Galley Spindle (#S1)	1⅛"
2	*Screw Eye (#3290)	1⁹⁄₁₆"

*Available from Meisel Hardware Specialties.

Date Due:
Tuesday
May 7
2013

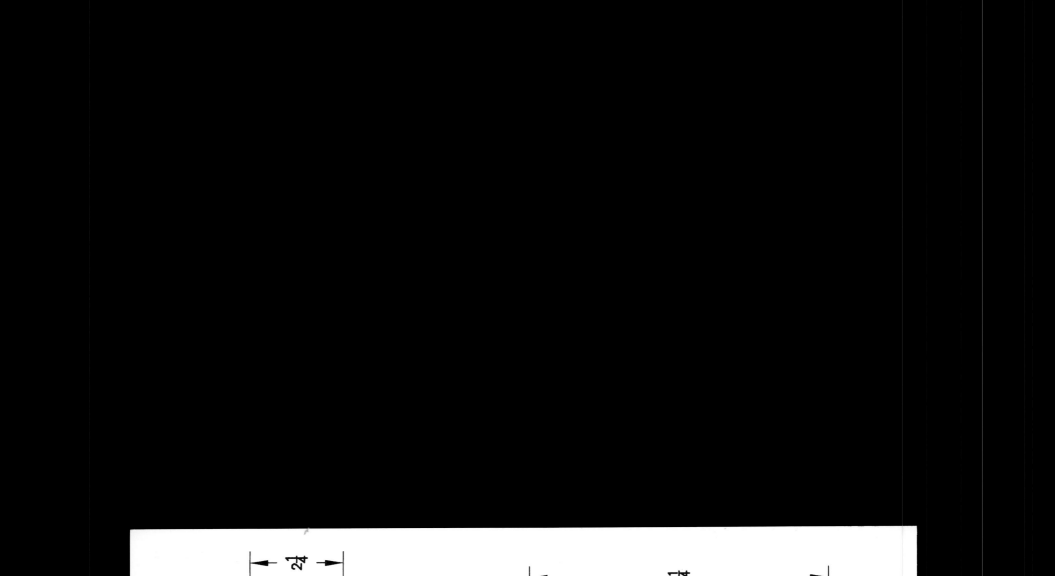

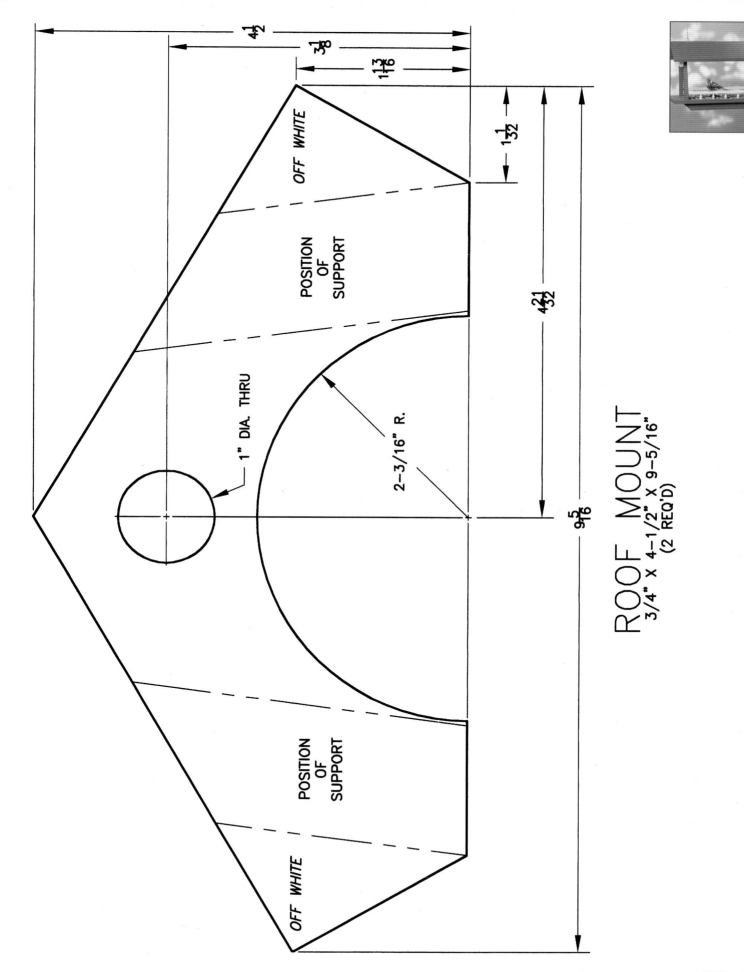

ROOF MOUNT
3/4" X 4–1/2" X 9–5/16"
(2 REQ'D)

OFF WHITE

POSITION OF SUPPORT

1" DIA. THRU

2–3/16" R.

POSITION OF SUPPORT

OFF WHITE

$4\frac{1}{2}$

$3\frac{3}{8}$

$1\frac{13}{16}$

$1\frac{1}{32}$

$4\frac{21}{32}$

$9\frac{5}{16}$

Flutterby Birdfeeder

The name "flutterby" is a play on the word fairy and the word butterfly. I used the name for this birdfeeder because the two fairies on the birdfeeder have been designed to resemble the shape of a butterfly.

Although this birdfeeder is quite decorative, the design is actually very simple. A scroll saw is used to cut the fairies from a piece of ½" exterior plywood. The seed tray is a simple rectangular frame made from four pieces of 2x2 stock. The post is also a length of 2x2. A piece of window screen is nailed to the bottom of the seed tray.

The simplicity of the design carries through to the paint. The entire project, with the exception of the window screen, is painted white.

PLAN OF PROCEDURE

Fairies: A scroll saw is used to cut the Fairy pieces. Use ½" exterior plywood. The Fairies pattern is drawn full size; however, it is presented on two pages because of the large size. All lines are cut lines. For each of the inside cuts, you will need to drill small holes, thread the scroll saw blade through and then cut the detail. The cut lines should be about $1/16$" thick so that the detail can be seen from a distance.

Because scroll saw blades are typically very narrow, it will be necessary to make two cuts very close to each other to create the desired width. Cut these detail lines about $1/16$" wide. The wide cut lines will be less likely to fill with paint.

Feed Tray: Cut the feed tray Front, Back and Side pieces from 2x2 stock. Miter the ends 45 degrees. They can be assembled with glue and reinforced with nails or screws. The 2x2 Post is screwed to the outside of the Back piece of the feed tray. This leaves the bottom of the feed tray fully open for the attachment of the Screen. Use Window Screen such as that sold in hardware stores. The bottom of the Post can be buried in the ground.

Fairies: Transfer the pattern onto ½" plywood and cut out.

Front/Back: Lay out and cut to size from 1½" stock. Cut the 45-degree miters. (One Front and One Back Piece Required)

Side: Lay out and cut to size from 1½" stock. Cut the 45-degree miters. (Two Pieces Required)

Post: Cut to size from 1½" stock. A suggested length is given in the Bill of Materials.

Wire Window Screen: Lay out and cut to the size given in the Bill of Materials.

FINAL ASSEMBLY

Assemble the Front, the Back and the Side pieces as shown in the illustration. Attach the Fairies to the inside of the tray assembly. Attach the mitered tray assembly to the Post. Attach the Wire Window Screen to the bottom of the mitered box assembly with a staple gun. Insert the Post in the ground to display the finished project.

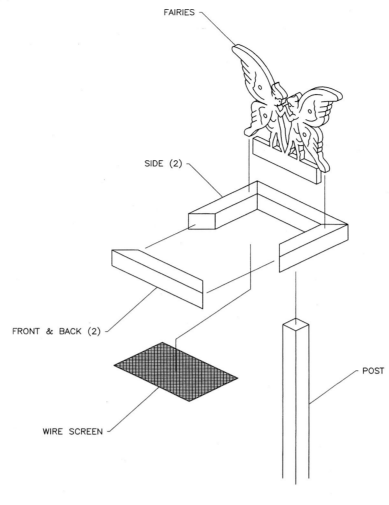

FAIRIES

SIDE (2)

FRONT & BACK (2)

POST

WIRE SCREEN

ASSEMBLY DRAWING

FLUTTERBY BIRDFEEDER: BILL OF MATERIALS

Quantity	Description	Size of Material
1	Fairies	$\frac{1}{2}$" x $9\frac{5}{8}$" x 12"
2	Front/Back	$1\frac{1}{2}$" x $1\frac{1}{2}$" x $10\frac{1}{4}$"
2	Side	$1\frac{1}{2}$" x $1\frac{1}{2}$" x $7\frac{3}{4}$"
1	Post	$1\frac{1}{2}$" x $1\frac{1}{2}$" x 60" (not drawn)
1	Wire Window Screen	$6\frac{3}{4}$" x $9\frac{1}{4}$"

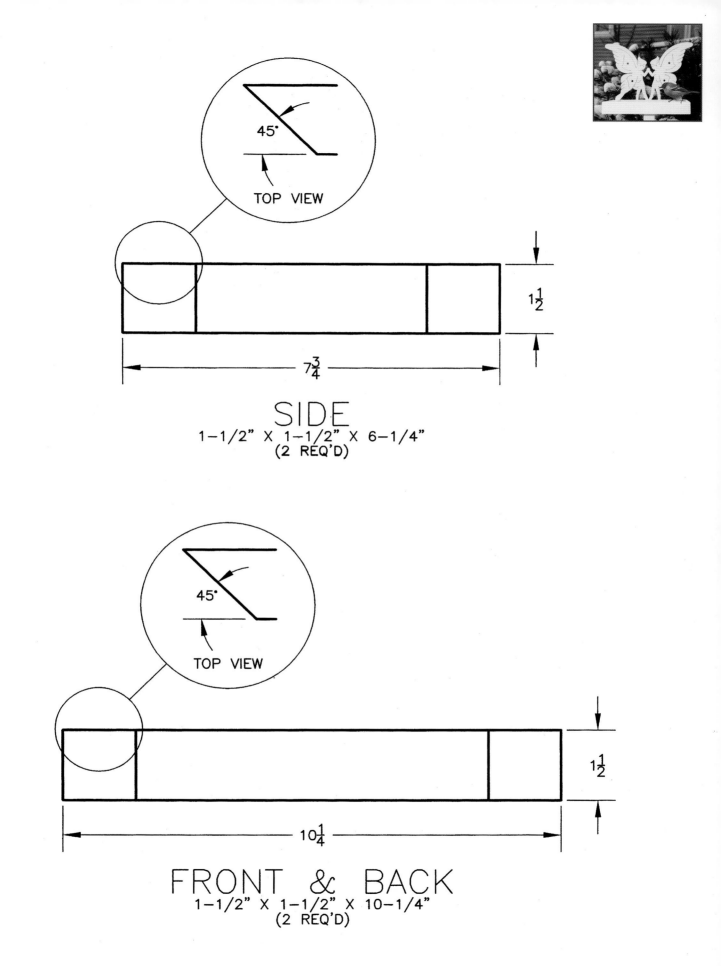

45°

TOP VIEW

$1\frac{1}{2}$

$7\frac{3}{4}$

SIDE
1–1/2" X 1–1/2" X 6–1/4"
(2 REQ'D)

45°

TOP VIEW

$1\frac{1}{2}$

$10\frac{1}{4}$

FRONT & BACK
1–1/2" X 1–1/2" X 10–1/4"
(2 REQ'D)

Cutting Pattern (100%)

FAIRIES
1/2" X 9-5/8" X 12"

Cutting Pattern (100%)
FAIRIES
1/2" X 9–5/8" X 12"

Gazebo Birdfeeder

This birdfeeder incorporates several pleasing features, including ivy leaf scrollwork and an all-white painted finish. Most parts are cut from ½" exterior plywood, so the project is inexpensive to make.

The edges of the side pieces are cut with 45-degree bevels so that when they are glued together, the edges of the plywood will be hidden.

For simplicity of construction, the roof pieces do not require bevels. When the roof pieces are assembled, the gaps where the roof boards meet are covered with wood dowels.

A 10"-diameter plastic or clay pottery tray is set inside the project to hold the bird food. Use the type of tray commonly sold for drip trays under large clay flowerpots. They are available at lawn and garden centers and greenhouses. The tray diameter must not be larger than the 10½" access hole in the side pieces.

PLAN OF PROCEDURE

This project is constructed from ½" exterior plywood. Waterproof glue is recommended for outdoor use. Joints should be reinforced with nails or screws.

Roof Trim: Lay out and cut to size from ½" stock.

Bottom Trim: Lay out and cut to size from ½" stock. Cut the 45-degree bevels. Transfer the pattern with carbon paper and cut out. (Four Pieces Required)

Roof Support #1 and #2: Lay out and cut to size from ½" stock. (One of Each Piece Required)

Roof: Lay out and cut to size from ½" stock. (Four Pieces Required)

Side: Lay out and cut to size from ½" stock. Cut the 45-degree bevels. Trace the pattern with carbon paper and cut out. (Four Pieces Required)

Top/Bottom: Lay out and cut to size from ½" stock. Drill the ¼" drain holes. (One Top and One Bottom Piece Required)

Dowel: Cut to length from ½" dowel stock according to the length given in the Bill of Materials.

Wood Ball: Sand a 1"-diameter flat spot on one side of the 3" Wood Ball.

FINAL ASSEMBLY

Step 1: Assemble the Side pieces. Assemble the Bottom Trim pieces. Attach the Bottom piece. Attach the Top to the Side Assembly. Attach Roof Support #1 and Roof Support #2 to the Top.

Step 2: Attach the Wood Ball to the Roof Trim with the 1¾" x #10 Wood Screw. Attach the Roof Trim and the Roof pieces to the Roof Supports. Bevel the ends of the Dowels to match the Roof Trim. Glue the Dowels in the creases formed by the Roof pieces.

Step 3: Paint the entire project white. Insert the Screw Eye into the Wood Ball in order to hang the project. Alternately, the project may be mounted on a wood post. Place the Birdfeeder Saucer inside the project.

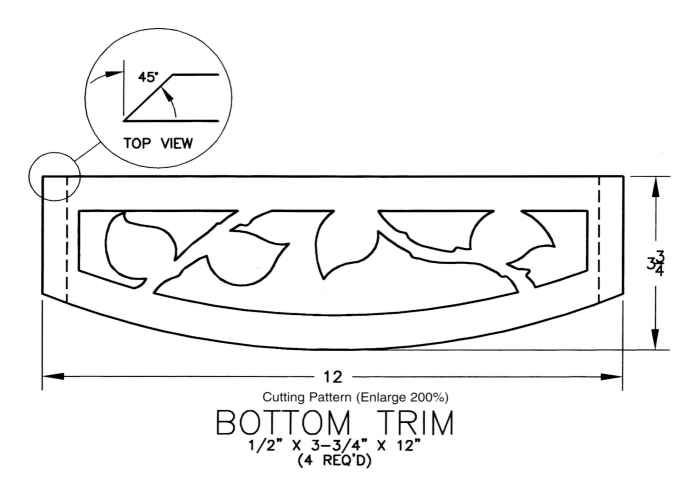

45°

TOP VIEW

Cutting Pattern (Enlarge 200%)

BOTTOM TRIM
1/2" X 3-3/4" X 12"
(4 REQ'D)

12

3¾

GAZEBO BIRDFEEDER: BILL OF MATERIALS

Quantity	Description	Size of Material
1	Roof Trim	½" x 3½" x 3½"
4	Bottom Trim	½" x 3¾" x 12"
1	Roof Support #1	½" x 6¼" x 13½"
1	Roof Support #2	½" x 6¼" x 13½"
4	Roof	½" x 9¼" x 14¾"
4	Side	½" x 12" x 14"
2	Top/Bottom	½" x 13½" x 13½"
4	Dowel	½" dia. x 11¼"
1	Birdfeeder Saucer	10"
1	*Screw Eye (#3290)	1⁹⁄₁₆"
1	*Wood Screw (#WS13410)	1¾" x #10
1	*Wood Ball (#1350)	3" dia.

*Available from Meisel Hardware Specialties.

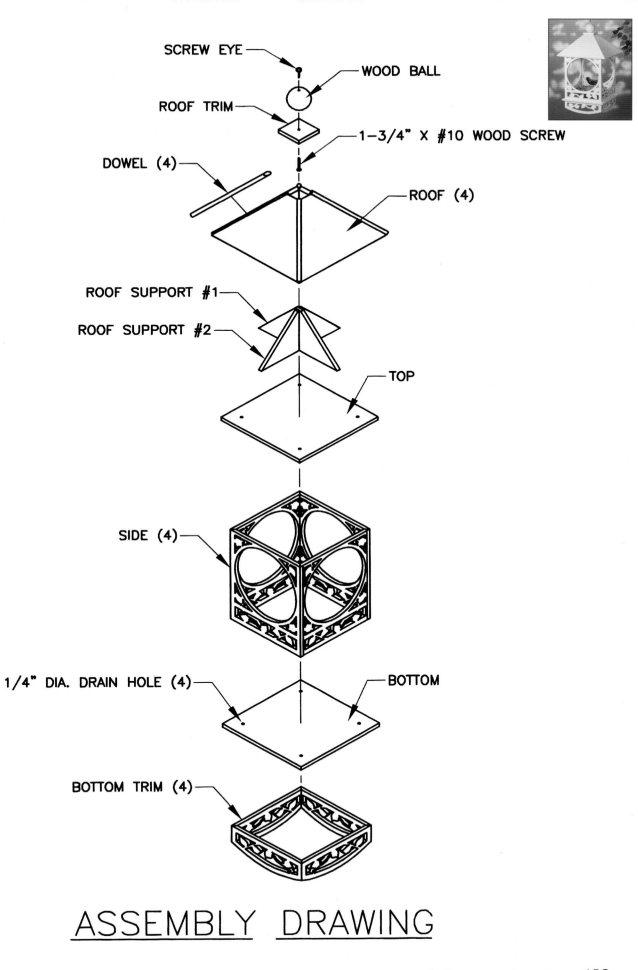

SCREW EYE

WOOD BALL

ROOF TRIM

1-3/4" X #10 WOOD SCREW

DOWEL (4)

ROOF (4)

ROOF SUPPORT #1

ROOF SUPPORT #2

TOP

SIDE (4)

1/4" DIA. DRAIN HOLE (4)

BOTTOM

BOTTOM TRIM (4)

ASSEMBLY DRAWING

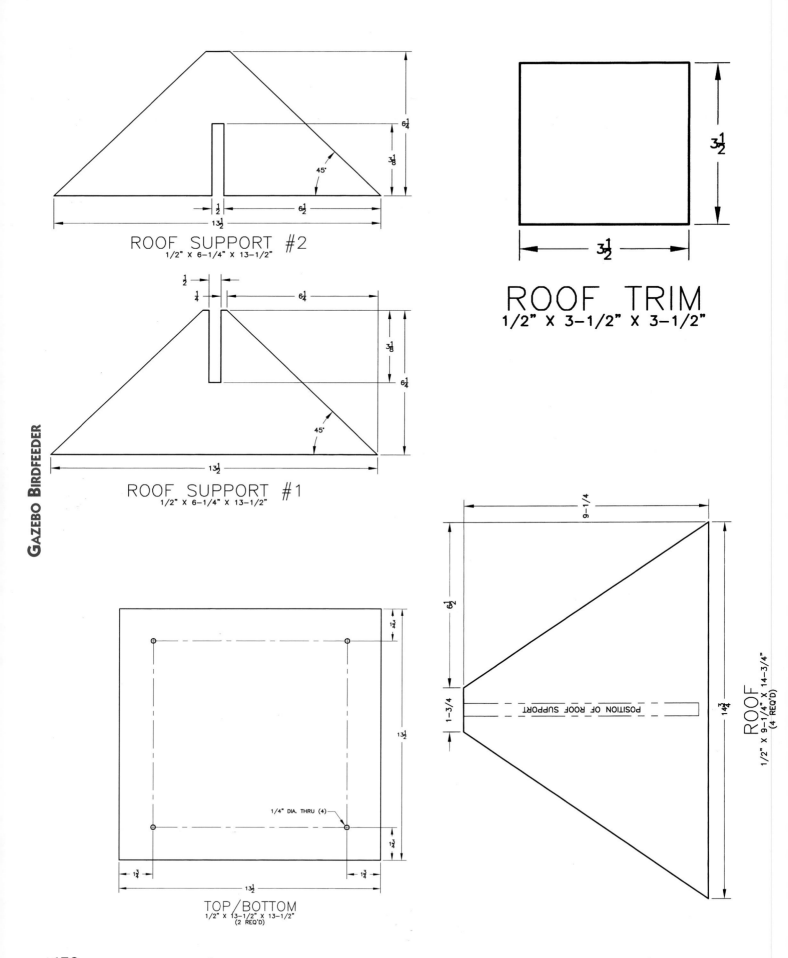

ROOF SUPPORT #2
1/2" X 6-1/4" X 13-1/2"

ROOF SUPPORT #1
1/2" X 6-1/4" X 13-1/2"

ROOF TRIM
1/2" X 3-1/2" X 3-1/2"

ROOF
1/2" X 9-1/4" X 14-3/4"
(4 REQ'D)

POSITION OF ROOF SUPPORT

1/4" DIA. THRU (4)

TOP/BOTTOM
1/2" X 13-1/2" X 13-1/2"
(2 REQ'D)

GAZEBO BIRDFEEDER

45°

TOP VIEW

14

12

Cutting Pattern (Enlarge 200%)

SIDE
1/2" X 12" X 14"
(4 REQ'D)

Local Feed Supply

When I was young, there was a popular cartoon show called "The Heckle and Jeckle Show." Heckle and Jeckle were two magpies. Magpies are from the crow family. As I recall it was a pretty good cartoon show. I had Heckle and Jeckle in the back of my mind when I designed this bird feeder. I guess it has been about forty years since I last watched this cartoon show. Maybe some of you remember the show, too. If you don't like crows but love sunflowers, try making this birdfeeder without the crow cutout.

PLAN OF PROCEDURE

This project uses ¼" exterior plywood and ¾" stock. By layering the plywood pieces, dimension is added. It is best to use a very good grade of exterior plywood. You will need one square foot of ¼" plywood. The screen on the bottom is common window screen. Check your local hardware store. Either fiberglass or metal screen is satisfactory.

Dowel: Cut to length from ¼" diameter Dowel stock according to the dimensions given in the Bill of Materials.

Crow Body, Wings, Fingers and Leg: Transfer the patterns to ¼" plywood and cut out.

Screen Cleat: Layout and cut to size from ¾" stock according to the dimensions given in the Bill of Materials.

Sign: Transfer the pattern and hole positions to ¾" stock and cut out. Drill the ¼" diameter x ⅜" deep hole on center where shown.

Sunflower Front: Enlarge on a photo copier, transfer the pattern and hole positions to ¾" stock and cut out. Drill the ¼" dia x ⅜" deep hole where shown. Do not drill the ⁷⁄₆₄" dia x ⅞" deep pilot holes until you are ready to assemble the project.

Sunflower Back: Enlarge on a photo copier, then transfer the pattern and hole positions to ¾" stock and cut out. Drill the ⁹⁄₆₄" diameter holes and countersink the holes for screws.

Screen: Layout and cut to the size given in the Bill of Materials. The screen is a half circle. Draw a 4⅜" radius half circle with a compass and cut out.

Sand all parts.

FINAL ASSEMBLY

It is easiest to paint some pieces before assembly, but since glue does not adhere well to painted surfaces, care should be taken to leave at least some exposed wood in areas where pieces will be glued together.

For example, place the Crow Body on the Sunflower Back in the location shown on the drawing and mark this location with a sharp pencil. Do not paint the areas where these pieces will be glued to each other. In this way, the Crow Body can be glued to the Sunflower Back after both pieces are painted. This makes painting much easier.

Glue the Screen Cleat to the Sunflower Back where shown. Attach the Sunflower Front to the Sunflower Back with the 1⅝" screws. Attach the Screen to the bottom of the Sunflower Front and Screen Cleat with a staple gun.

Glue the Dowel in the ¼" diameter holes in the Sign and Sunflower Front. Glue the Crow Wings to the Sunflower Back. Glue the Crow Body and Crow Fingers to the Crow Wings. Glue the Crow Leg to the Crow Body.

The finished project may be attached to a stake and displayed in the yard or attached directly to the side of a house or tree.

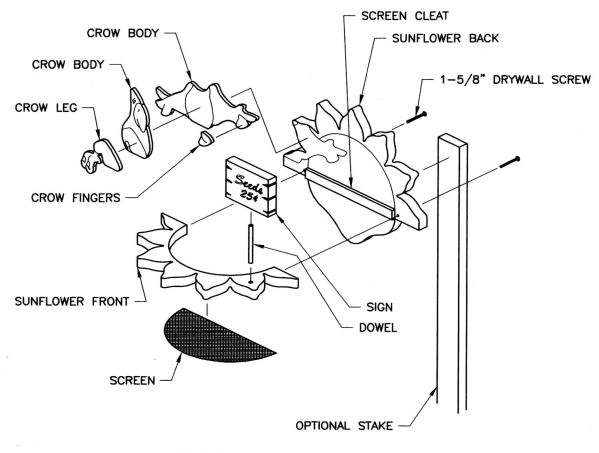

CROW BODY

CROW BODY

CROW LEG

CROW FINGERS

SCREEN CLEAT

SUNFLOWER BACK

1–5/8" DRYWALL SCREW

SUNFLOWER FRONT

SIGN

DOWEL

SCREEN

OPTIONAL STAKE

ASSEMBLY DRAWING

LOCAL FEED SUPPLY: BILL OF MATERIALS

Quantity	Description	Size of Material
1	Dowel	¼" dia x 3" (not drawn)
1	Crow Fingers	¼" 1⅛" x 1¼"
1	Crow Body	¼" x 2¾" x 5¼"
1	Crow Leg	¼" x 3¼" x 3¾"
1	Crow Wings	¼" x 4½" x 9⅝"
1	Screen Cleat	¼" x ¾" x 8¼" (not drawn)
1	Sign	¾" x 3" x 4"
1	Sunflower Front	¾" x 6½" x 12⅞"
1	Sunflower Back	¾" x 10⅞" x 12⅞"
1	Screen	4⅜" x 8¾"
2	Screw	1⅝" x #6

LOCAL FEED SUPPLY

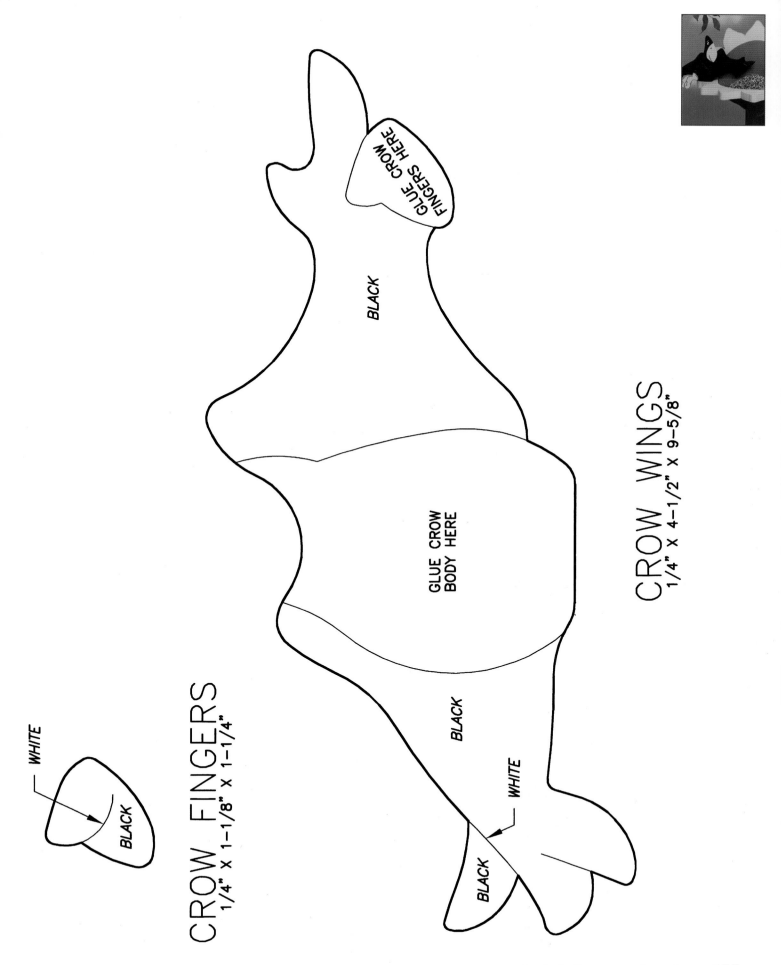

CROW WINGS
1/4" x 4-1/2" x 9-5/8"

GLUE CROW
FINGERS HERE

BLACK

GLUE CROW
BODY HERE

BLACK

WHITE

BLACK

CROW FINGERS
1/4" x 1-1/8" x 1-1/4"

WHITE

BLACK

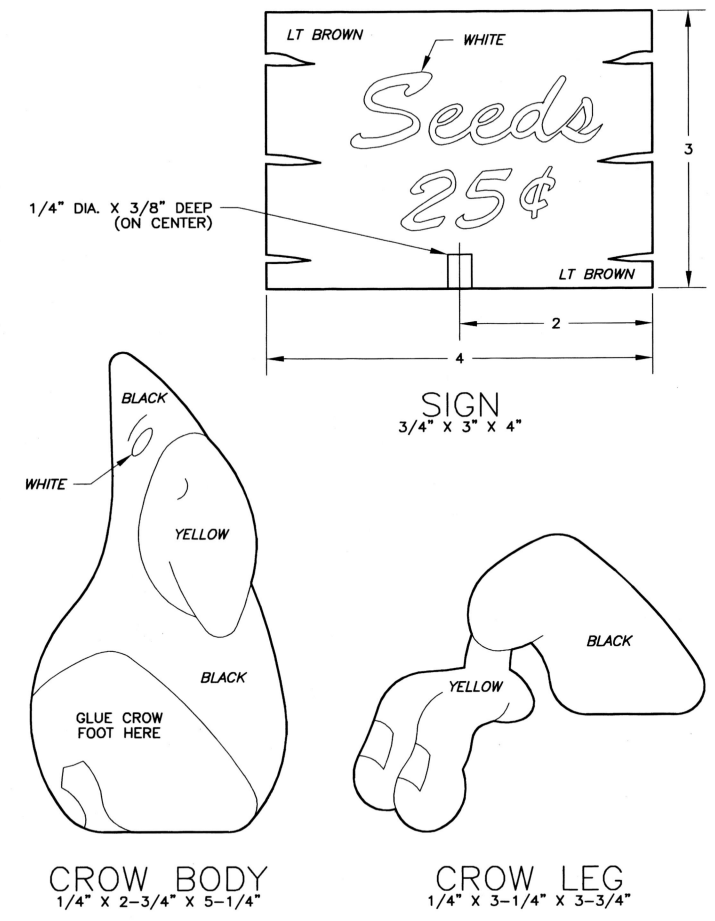

LT BROWN

WHITE

Seeds
25¢

1/4" DIA. X 3/8" DEEP
(ON CENTER)

LT BROWN

3

2

4

SIGN
3/4" X 3" X 4"

BLACK

WHITE

YELLOW

BLACK

GLUE CROW
FOOT HERE

BLACK

YELLOW

CROW BODY
1/4" X 2-3/4" X 5-1/4"

CROW LEG
1/4" X 3-1/4" X 3-3/4"

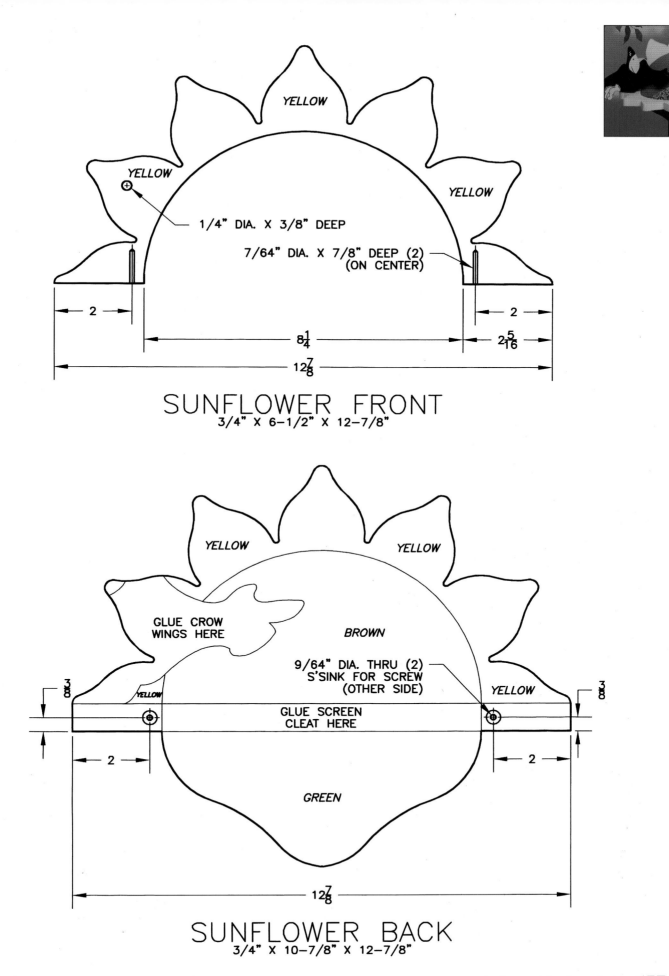

YELLOW

YELLOW

YELLOW

1/4" DIA. X 3/8" DEEP

7/64" DIA. X 7/8" DEEP (2)
(ON CENTER)

2

$8\frac{1}{4}$

$2\frac{5}{16}$

$12\frac{7}{8}$

SUNFLOWER FRONT
3/4" X 6-1/2" X 12-7/8"

YELLOW

YELLOW

GLUE CROW
WINGS HERE

BROWN

9/64" DIA. THRU (2)
S'SINK FOR SCREW
(OTHER SIDE)

YELLOW

YELLOW

GLUE SCREEN
CLEAT HERE

3/4

3/4

2

2

GREEN

$12\frac{7}{8}$

SUNFLOWER BACK
3/4" X 10-7/8" X 12-7/8"

Mallard Birdfeeder

Hopper style birdfeeders are very practical. A hinged lid on each side keeps rain out and provides easy access for filling the feeder.

The thing that struck me about most feeders of this type was that there simply wasn't much imagination given to the style. So for this project, I designed the hinged lids in the shape of wings. Then by cutting the top piece in the shape of a duck, the project took on its own character.

This one is painted like a mallard duck; however, if you check the color pictures in a good bird book, you could paint this project to look like other species of ducks as well.

Plan of Procedure

This project can be built from pine, cedar or redwood. Most parts are cut from ¾" thick material. The Perch that runs along each Side of the project is made from a ⅝" birch Dowel. These Perches are attached with ¼" dowel pins that are 2" long.

Drawings are not provided for the Hopper Spacers or the Bottom piece since they are simple rectangular-shaped pieces.

Hopper: Lay out and cut to size from ¾" stock. Cut the ⅛"-wide x ¼" deep grooves. (Two Pieces Required)

Side: Enlarge the pattern and transfer it to ¾" stock and cut out. (Two Pieces Required)

Hopper Spacer: Lay out and cut to size from ¾" stock according to the dimensions given in the Bill of Materials. (Two Pieces Required)

Bottom: Lay out and cut to size from ¾" stock according to the dimensions given in the Bill of Materials.

Perch: Cut to length from ⅝" Dowel stock. Drill ¼" diameter holes where shown. (Two Pieces Required)

Bottom Side: Lay out and cut to size from ¾" stock. Drill the ¼" diameter holes. (Two Pieces Required)

Mallard: Enlarge the pattern 200%, transfer it to ¾" stock and cut out.

Wing: Lay out and cut stock to rough size from ¾" stock. Cut the 45-degree bevel. Enlarge the pattern 200% and transfer to your stock. Note: There is a right-hand and a left-hand piece. Cut where shown to the separate edge of the Wing and re-attach the Wing using Hinges.

Final Assembly

Step 1: Attach the Bottom, the Hopper Spacer and the Hopper pieces to the Sides in the position shown on the drawing of the Side piece. Assemble the Bottom Sides, the Perch Dowels and the Perches. Attach the Bottom Sides to the Bottom, flush with the Bottom edge.

Step 2: Slip the Hopper Side pieces in the ⅛" x ¼" deep grooves in the Hopper pieces. Attach the Mallard to the Side pieces. Attach the Wings to the Sides and the Mallard. The cut Wing pieces are attached with Hinges to provide access for refilling the feeder.

Step 3: Insert Screw Eyes into the top edge of the Mallard in order to hang the project. Alternately, the project may be mounted on a post attached to the Bottom.

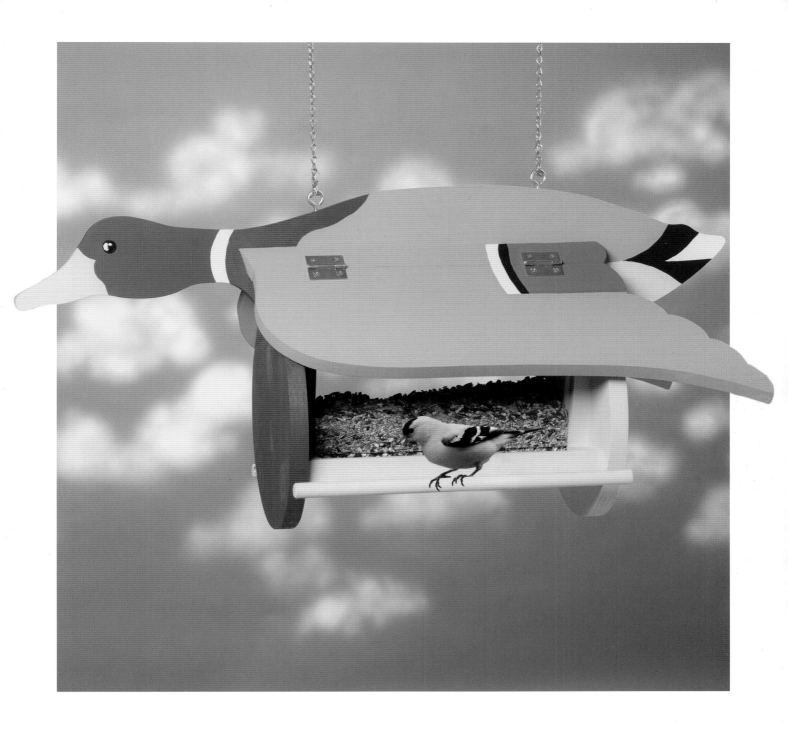

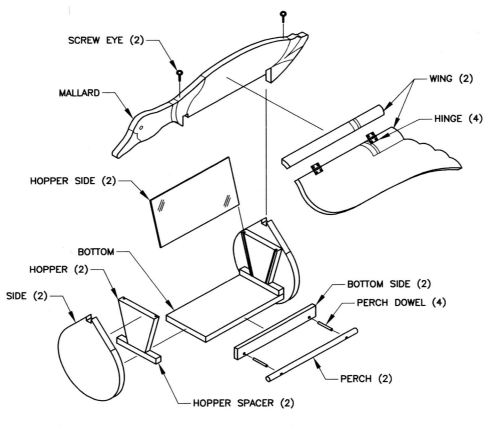

SCREW EYE (2)

MALLARD

WING (2)

HINGE (4)

HOPPER SIDE (2)

BOTTOM
HOPPER (2)
SIDE (2)

BOTTOM SIDE (2)
PERCH DOWEL (4)

PERCH (2)

HOPPER SPACER (2)

ASSEMBLY DRAWING

MALLARD BIRDFEEDER: BILL OF MATERIALS

Quantity	Description	Size of Material
2	Hopper	¾" x 5⅜" x 5½"
2	Side	¾" x 9⅜" x 11"
2	Hopper Spacer	¾" x ¾" x 6" (not drawn)
1	Bottom	¾" x 6" x 12" (not drawn)
2	Perch	⅝" dia. x 13½" dowel
2	Bottom Side	½" x 1½" x 12"
1	Mallard	¾" x 6⅜" x 29⅜"
2	Wing	¾" x 9⅛" x 20⅛"
2	*Hopper Side (#1377)	⅛" x 5⅜" x 11" Clear Acrylic
4	*Perch Dowel (#1142)	¼" dia. x 2"
4	*Hinge (#1276)	1½" x 1½"
2	*Screw Eye (#3290)	1⁹⁄₁₆"

*Available from Meisel Hardware Specialties.

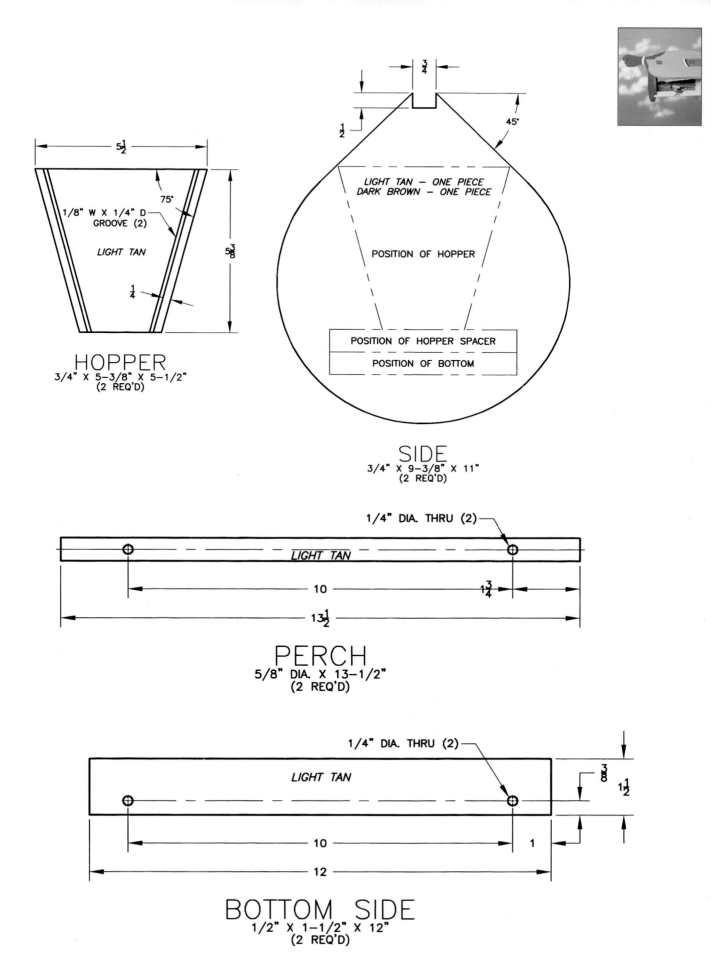

HOPPER
3/4" X 5-3/8" X 5-1/2"
(2 REQ'D)

5½

75°

1/8" W X 1/4" D
GROOVE (2)

LIGHT TAN

5⅜

¼

¾

½

45°

LIGHT TAN — ONE PIECE
DARK BROWN — ONE PIECE

POSITION OF HOPPER

POSITION OF HOPPER SPACER

POSITION OF BOTTOM

SIDE
3/4" X 9-3/8" X 11"
(2 REQ'D)

1/4" DIA. THRU (2)

LIGHT TAN

10

1¾

13½

PERCH
5/8" DIA. X 13-1/2"
(2 REQ'D)

1/4" DIA. THRU (2)

LIGHT TAN

⅜

1½

10

1

12

BOTTOM SIDE
1/2" X 1-1/2" X 12"
(2 REQ'D)

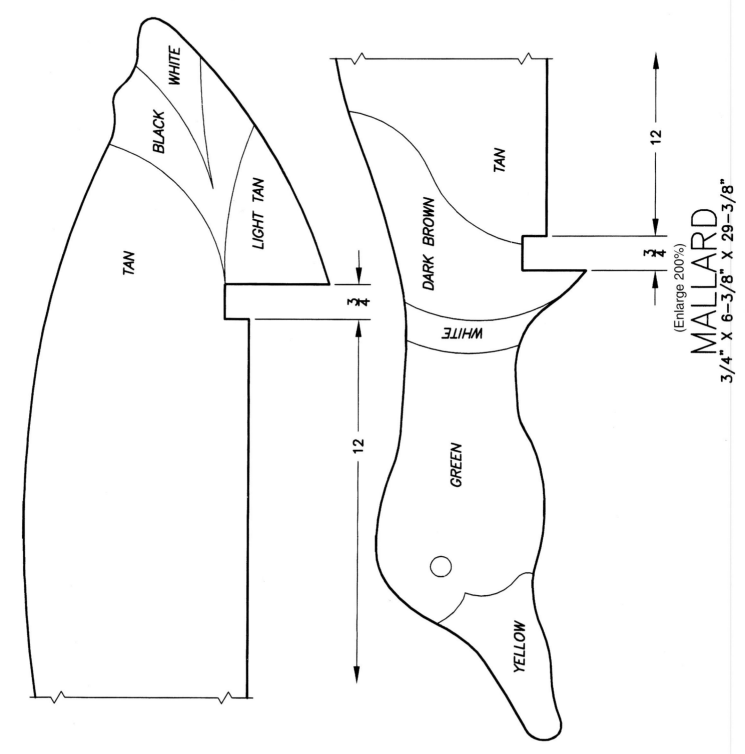

MALLARD
3/4" x 6-3/8" x 29-3/8"
(Enlarge 200%)

TAN

BLACK

WHITE

LIGHT TAN

3/4

12

DARK BROWN

TAN

WHITE

GREEN

YELLOW

3/4

12

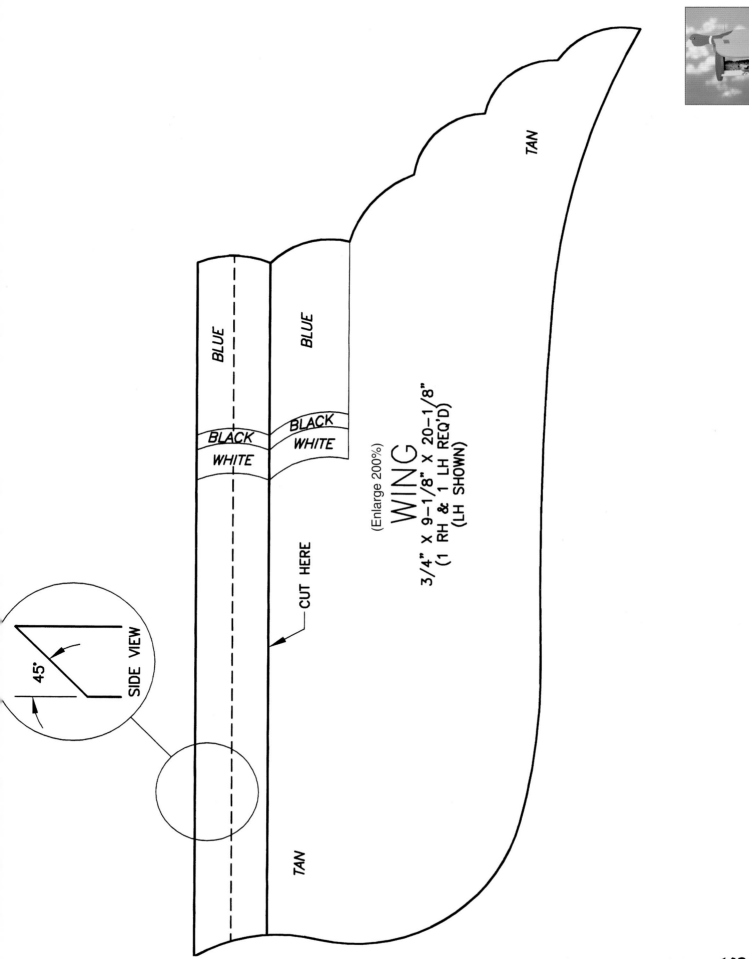

TAN

BLUE

BLUE

BLACK

BLACK

WHITE

WHITE

(Enlarge 200%)
WING
3/4" X 9–1/8" X 20–1/8"
(1 RH & 1 LH REQ'D)
(LH SHOWN)

CUT HERE

TAN

45°

SIDE VIEW

TAN

Sleeping Cat Birdfeeder

This decorative birdfeeder features an optional sleeping cat inside. This visual element brings a smile to humans, yet does not seem to unnerve live birds, which are quite happy to visit the feeder.

Build this feeder from standard pine or cedar boards. Cedar shakes on the roof contrast nicely with the white paint. Two brightly painted wooden birds add color and interest.

Mount the finished project on a sturdy 4x4 post at a height you can reach.

PLAN OF PROCEDURE

To build this open-style feeder, begin by cutting all pieces to size. The Cat Body, the Tail, the Leg and the Paws are drawn full size. Birds #1 and #2 are also drawn full size. These patterns can be transferred directly to your wood with carbon paper or transfer paper. The Side pieces need to be enlarged to make a full-size pattern. The drawings for the remaining parts, including the Base, the Base Front, the Base Back, the Base Sides and the Roof have been scaled down to fit on the pages. For these pieces, simply lay them out and cut them to size.

Paw: Transfer the patterns to ¾" stock and cut out. (Two Pieces Required)

Tail, Leg, Cat Body: Transfer the patterns to ¾" stock and cut out.

Bird #1 and #2: Transfer the patterns to ¾" stock and cut out. Drill the ¼" diameter x 1"-deep hole in each piece.

Base Front/Back, Base Side: Begin by cutting a strip of ¾" stock 1½" wide by approximately 62" long. Cut the ¾" wide x ¼" deep groove along the entire piece. Then cut the 45-degree angles on each piece. (Two Pieces of Each Required)

Side: Lay out and cut to size from ¾" stock. (Two Pieces Required)

Roof: Lay out and cut to size from ¾" stock. Cut the 45-degree angle on one edge. (Two Pieces Required)

Base: Lay out and cut to size from ¾" stock.

Dowel: Cut to length from ¼" dowel stock according to the Bill of Materials. (Two Pieces Required)

FINAL ASSEMBLY

Step 1: Attach the Paws and the Leg to the Cat Body where shown. Attach the Tail to the Leg where shown. Attach the Cat Assembly and the Side pieces to the Base in the position shown on the drawings of the Base piece. Attach the Base Front, the Base Back and the Base Sides to the Base. Attach the Roof pieces to the Side pieces where shown. Insert a Dowel in the ¼" holes in each of the Birds. Drill two ¼" diameter x ⅜" deep holes in the approximate positions shown in the Assembly Drawing and attach the Birds.

Step 2: You may choose to finish the Roof with cedar shakes. Cut 3"-long pieces from full-size cedar shakes and attach them to the Roof with exterior wood glue. Use a Black Paint Marker to add facial details to the Cat.

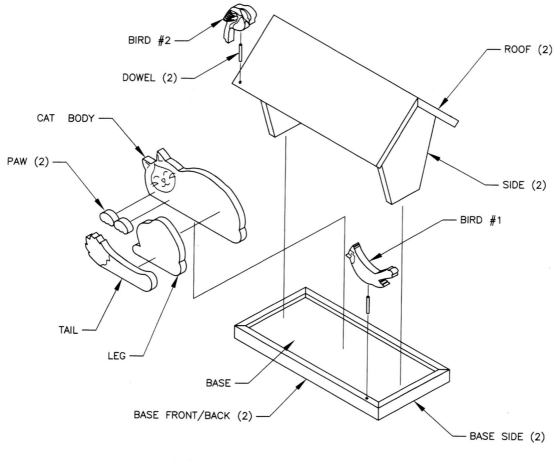

BIRD #2

DOWEL (2)

ROOF (2)

CAT BODY

PAW (2)

SIDE (2)

BIRD #1

TAIL

LEG

BASE

BASE FRONT/BACK (2)

BASE SIDE (2)

ASSEMBLY DRAWING

SLEEPING CAT FEEDER: BILL OF MATERIALS

Quantity	Description	Size of Material
2	Paw	¾" x 1¼" x 2"
2	Base Side	¾" x 1½" x 9¾"
2	Base Front/Back	¾" x 1½" x 20"
1	Tail	¾" x 3⅛" x 9¼"
1	Bird #1	¾" x 3¾" x 6½"
1	Bird #2	¾" x 3⅞" x 5¼"
1	Leg	¾" x 5¾" x 6¾"
1	Cat Body	¾" x 6¼" x 13¾"
2	Side	¾" x 8" x 12"
2	Roof	¾" x 8" x 20"
1	Base	¾" x 8¾" x 19"
2	Dowel	¼" dia. x 2" (not drawn)

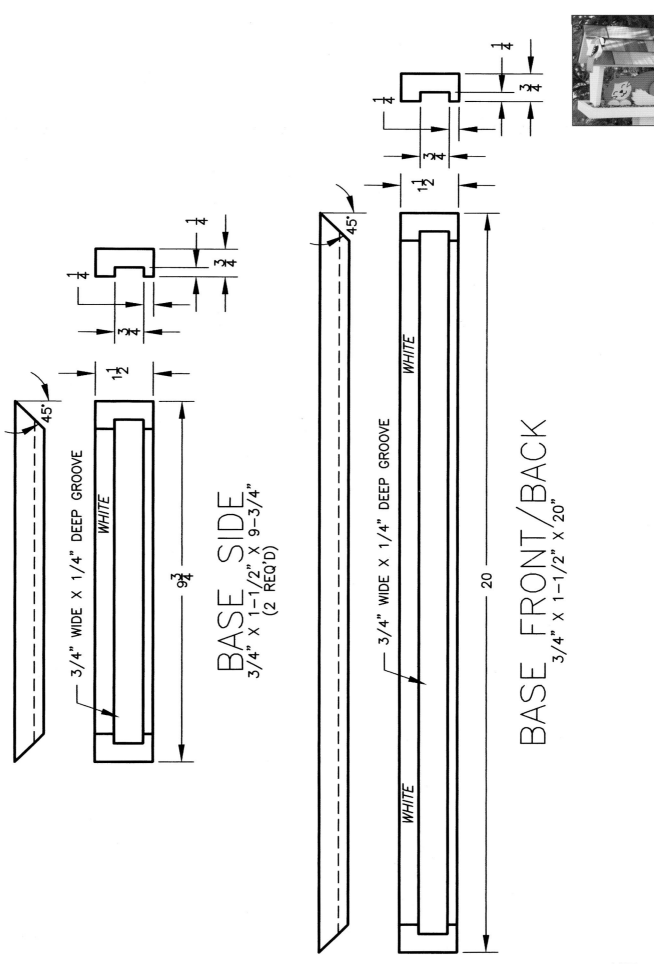

BASE SIDE
3/4" X 1-1/2" X 9-3/4"
(2 REQ'D)

3/4" WIDE X 1/4" DEEP GROOVE

WHITE

9¾

1½

¼

¾

¼

¾

45°

BASE FRONT/BACK
3/4" X 1-1/2" X 20"

3/4" WIDE X 1/4" DEEP GROOVE

WHITE

WHITE

20

1½

¼

¾

¼

¾

45°

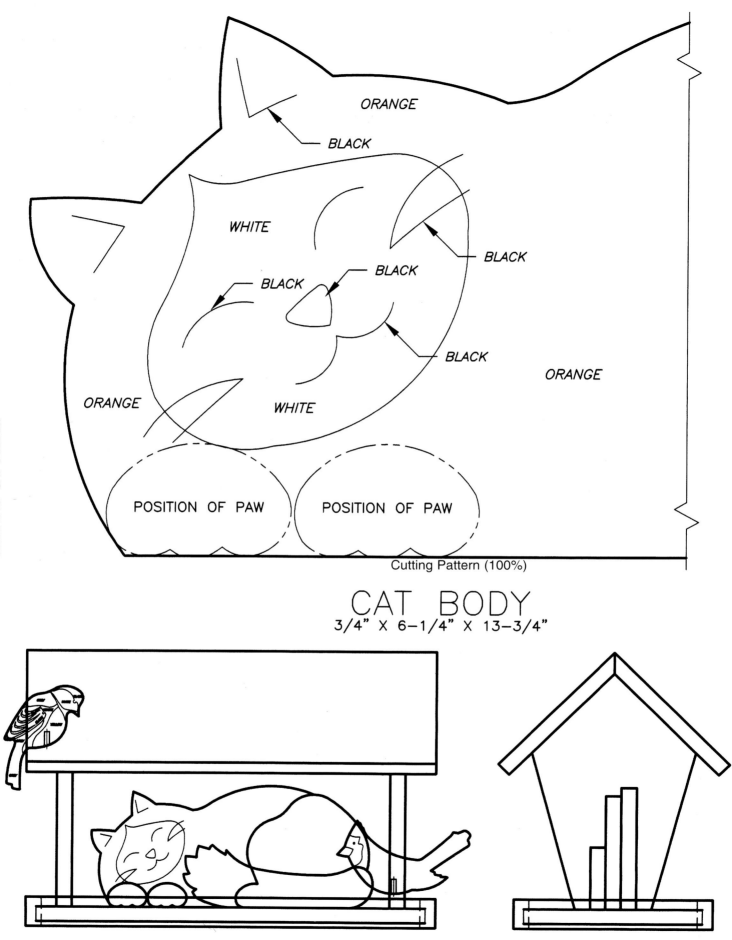

ORANGE

BLACK

WHITE

BLACK

BLACK

BLACK

BLACK

ORANGE

ORANGE

WHITE

POSITION OF PAW

POSITION OF PAW

Cutting Pattern (100%)

CAT BODY
3/4" X 6-1/4" X 13-3/4"

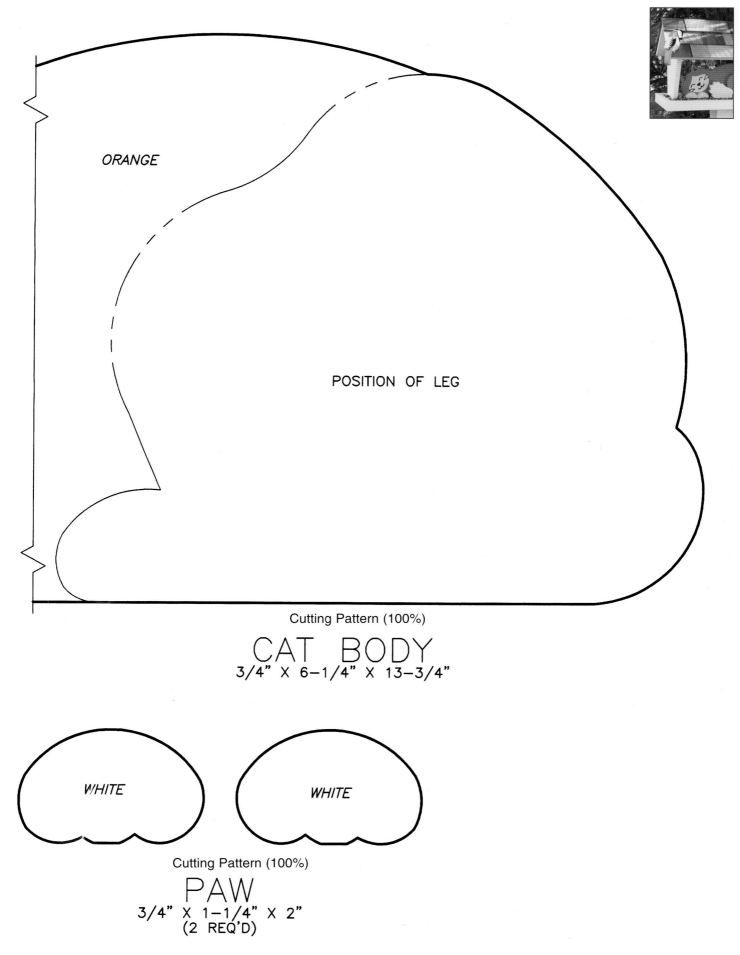

ORANGE

POSITION OF LEG

Cutting Pattern (100%)

CAT BODY
3/4" X 6-1/4" X 13-3/4"

WHITE   WHITE

Cutting Pattern (100%)

PAW
3/4" X 1-1/4" X 2"
(2 REQ'D)

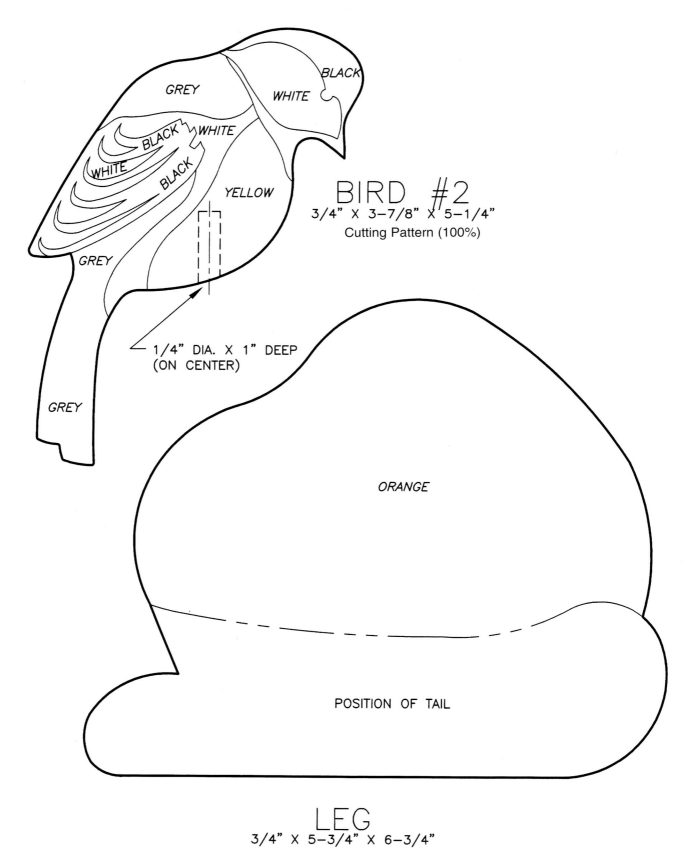

GREY

BLACK

WHITE

GREY

BLACK WHITE

WHITE

BLACK

YELLOW

GREY

BIRD #2

3/4" X 3-7/8" X 5-1/4"

Cutting Pattern (100%)

1/4" DIA. X 1" DEEP
(ON CENTER)

GREY

ORANGE

POSITION OF TAIL

LEG

3/4" X 5-3/4" X 6-3/4"

Cutting Pattern (100%)

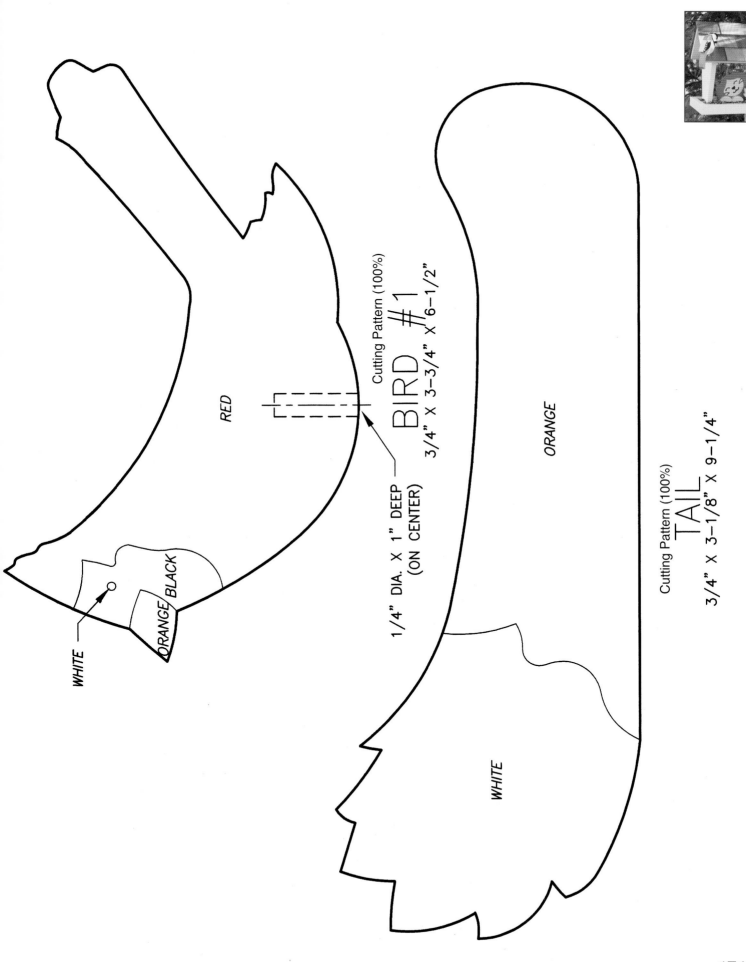

WHITE

ORANGE BLACK

RED

1/4" DIA. X 1" DEEP
(ON CENTER)

Cutting Pattern (100%)
BIRD #1
3/4" X 3-3/4" X 6-1/2"

ORANGE

Cutting Pattern (100%)
TAIL
3/4" X 3-1/8" X 9-1/4"

WHITE

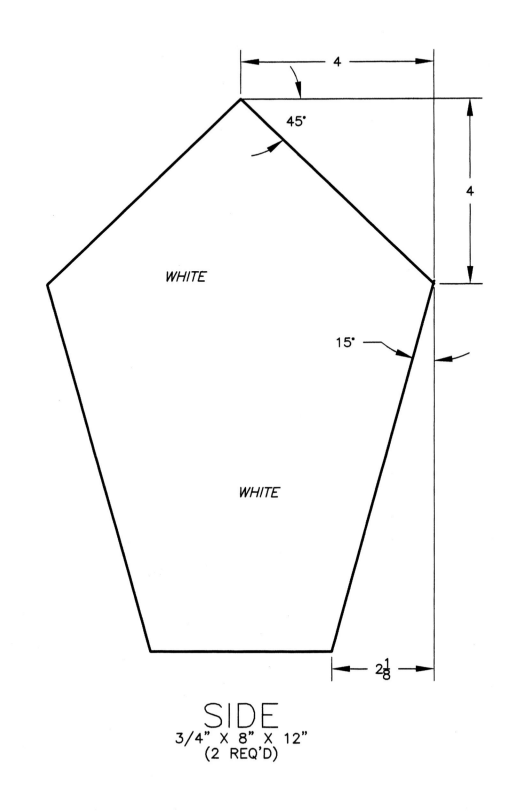

4

45°

WHITE

4

15°

WHITE

2$\frac{1}{8}$

SIDE
3/4" X 8" X 12"
(2 REQ'D)

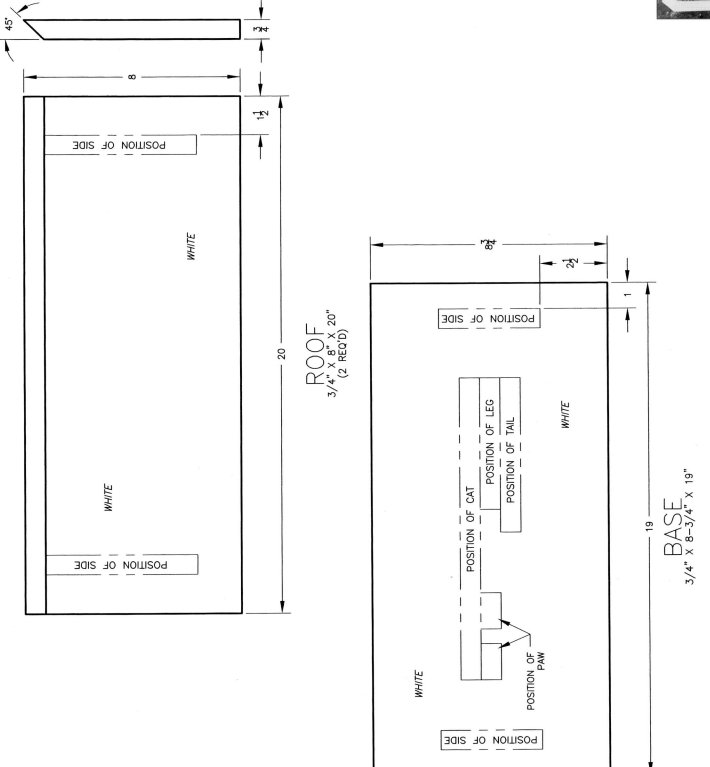

ROOF
3/4" X 8" X 20"
(2 REQ'D)

45°

3/4

8

1 1/2

POSITION OF SIDE

WHITE

WHITE

20

POSITION OF SIDE

BASE
3/4" X 8-3/4" X 19"

8 3/4

2 1/2

1

POSITION OF SIDE

POSITION OF CAT

POSITION OF LEG

POSITION OF TAIL

WHITE

POSITION OF PAW

WHITE

19

POSITION OF SIDE

Three Hummingbird Feeders

Three unique hummingbird feeders are presented in this chapter. The project on the right takes its design from the gingerbread that was often used to decorate Victorian homes. The feeder pictured in the center is more at home in the backyards of modern or contemporary homes. The feeder on the left has a decorative floral design, perfect for any style of home.

The plastic feeder bottle assemblies can be purchased as a unit. I've included a recipe for making your own liquid feed mixture, or you can buy commercially made hummingbird food.

Each of these products has been designed so that a portion of the feeder bottle will be visible. In this way, the liquid level can be easily monitored.

PLAN OF PROCEDURE

Each of these three projects is made in two sections. A 1/4" dowel holds the top section to the bottom section. By sliding the dowel out, the lower section can be removed to clean and refill the feeder bottle.

The side pieces on the Victorian and Floral feeders have 45-degree bevels on each side. The sides for both of these projects, as well as the Flower on the Floral feeder, are cut from 1/2" exterior plywood. The remaining pieces are cut from 3/4" solid stock.

The Modern feeder is made mostly from 3/4" solid stock. I used pine, but redwood and cedar are good choices as well.

Assembly is done with exterior glue and nails. See the Appendix for a parts package that consists of feeder bottles, dowels and screw eyes for three hummingbird feeders.

VICTORIAN AND FLORAL FEEDER

Flower (Floral feeder only): Transfer pattern to 1/2" plywood and cut out.

Side: Transfer pattern to 1/2" plywood and cut out. Cut bevels as shown. Drill the 5/16" diameter hole where shown on two pieces only. Cut out the scroll saw pattern (Four pieces required).

Hanging Bracket: Layout and cut to size from 3/4" stock. Drill 1/2" diameter hole.

Top: Layout and cut to size from 3/4" stock. Route chamfers on edges, if desired.

Wedge: Layout and cut to size from 3/4" stock. Drill the 5/16" diameter hole through. Sand the edges round on the two edges as shown.

Base: Layout and cut to size from 3/4" stock. Drill the 1" diameter hole through where shown. Cut the 1/4" x 1/4" chamfer around the inside of the 1" hole. On the Floral Base, cut the 45-degree bevel on one edge. Rout the chamfers as shown in the photograph if desired.

FINAL ASSEMBLY

Attach the Hanging Bracket to the top where shown. Attach the Top piece to the Wedge. Now is a good time to apply wood finish to those areas that will be difficult to reach after assembly. Glue the sides to each other as shown, being sure that the Side pieces with the 5/16" holes are opposite one another. Attach the Side assembly to the Base, making certain that the 5/16" holes are at the top. For the Floral Feeder, paint the Flower and attach it to the bevel on the base. Be sure that the 3/8" slot faces downward so that the feeder tube will pass through.

MODERN FEEDER

Hanging Bracket: Layout and cut to size from 3/4" stock. Drill the 1/2" diameter hole.

Mounting Bracket: Using a compass, layout a 2" diameter circle on 1 1/2" stock. Cut the circle shape to size and drill the 5/16" diameter hole through where shown.

Top: Layout and cut to size from 3/4" stock. Rout a 1/4" chamfer around the bottom edges, if desired. Cut the 2" diameter hole. Enlarge the hole slightly so that the 2" diameter Mounting Bracket will easily slip through. Drill 9/64" diameter shank clearance holes where shown.

Side: Layout and cut to size from ¾" stock. Cut the ¼" x ¼" bevel where shown. Drill the 7/64" diameter Pilot Holes on center where shown.

Base: Layout and cut to size from ¾" stock. Drill 1" diameter hole where shown. Cut the optional ¼" x ¼" chamfer, if desired.

FINAL ASSEMBLY

Attach the Hanging Bracket to the Mounting Bracket where shown. Screw the Sides to the Top with 1⅝" x #6 screws. Glue the Base to the Sides were shown.

FILLING YOUR FEEDER

Hummingbird food mixtures are available in many stores that sell bird food. However, you can make your own syrup by boiling 8 oz. of water for several minutes, then dissolving 1½ to 2 oz. of white sugar in the water. You may wish to add a few drops of red food coloring. Cool the mixture, and it's ready to use.

Fill the bottle completely before installing the stopper. This helps to avoid a lot of dripping, although a small amount of dripping is unavoidable.

Hang the feeder on a monofilament fishing line to prevent ants from crawling on the feeder.

THREE HUMMINGBIRD FEEDERS: BILL OF MATERIALS

Quantity	Description	Size of Material
Floral and Victorian Feeder: Bill of Materials		
1	Flower (Floral only)	½" x 4" x 4"
4	Side	½" x 3" x 6¾"
1	Hanging Bracket	¾" x 1¼" x 1⅝"
1	Top	¾" x 4" x 4"
1	Wedge	¾" x 2" x 2"
1	Base	¾" x 4" x 4"
Modern Feeder: Bill of Materials		
1	Hanging Bracket	¾" x 1¼" x 1⅝"
4	Side	¾" x ⅝" x 8"
1	Top	¾" x 4" x 4"
1	Base	¾" x 2" dia
1	Mounting Bracket	1½" x 2" dia
4	Screw (#1446)	2" x #6
For all Feeders (Hummingbird Feeder Hardware, #1225—See Appendix)		
3	Stopper/Tube/Cap	
3	Bottles	1 ⅞" dia x 6½"
3	Birch Dowels	¼" dia x 5"
3	Screw Eyes	

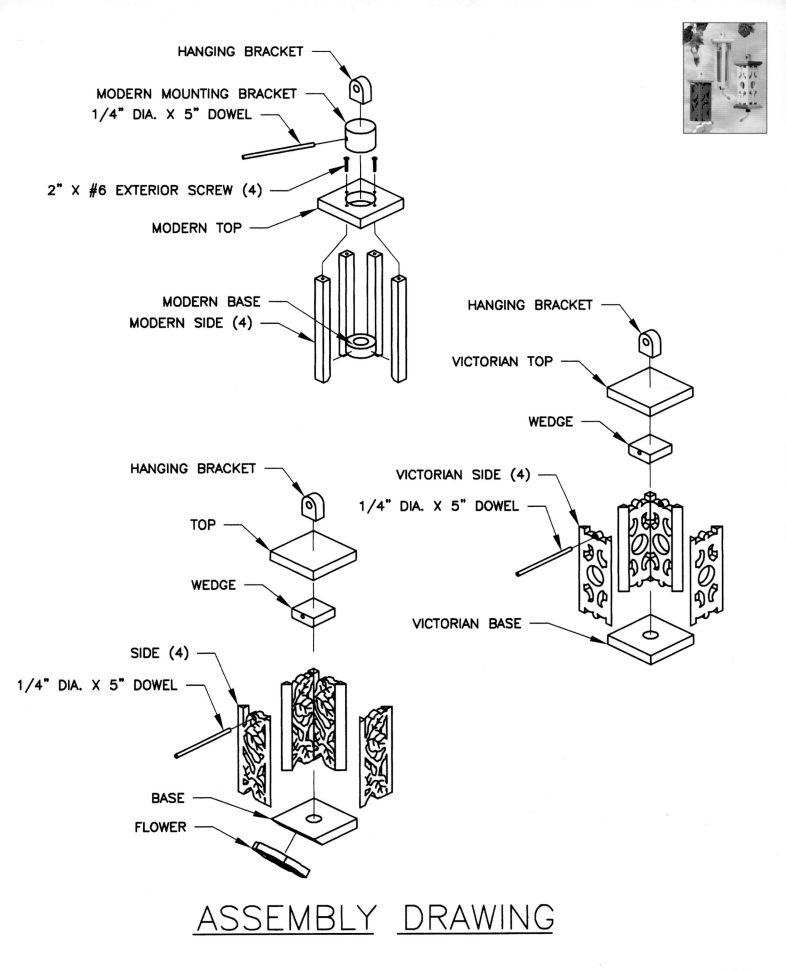

HANGING BRACKET

MODERN MOUNTING BRACKET

1/4" DIA. X 5" DOWEL

2" X #6 EXTERIOR SCREW (4)

MODERN TOP

MODERN BASE

MODERN SIDE (4)

HANGING BRACKET

VICTORIAN TOP

WEDGE

VICTORIAN SIDE (4)

1/4" DIA. X 5" DOWEL

VICTORIAN BASE

HANGING BRACKET

TOP

WEDGE

SIDE (4)

1/4" DIA. X 5" DOWEL

BASE

FLOWER

ASSEMBLY DRAWING

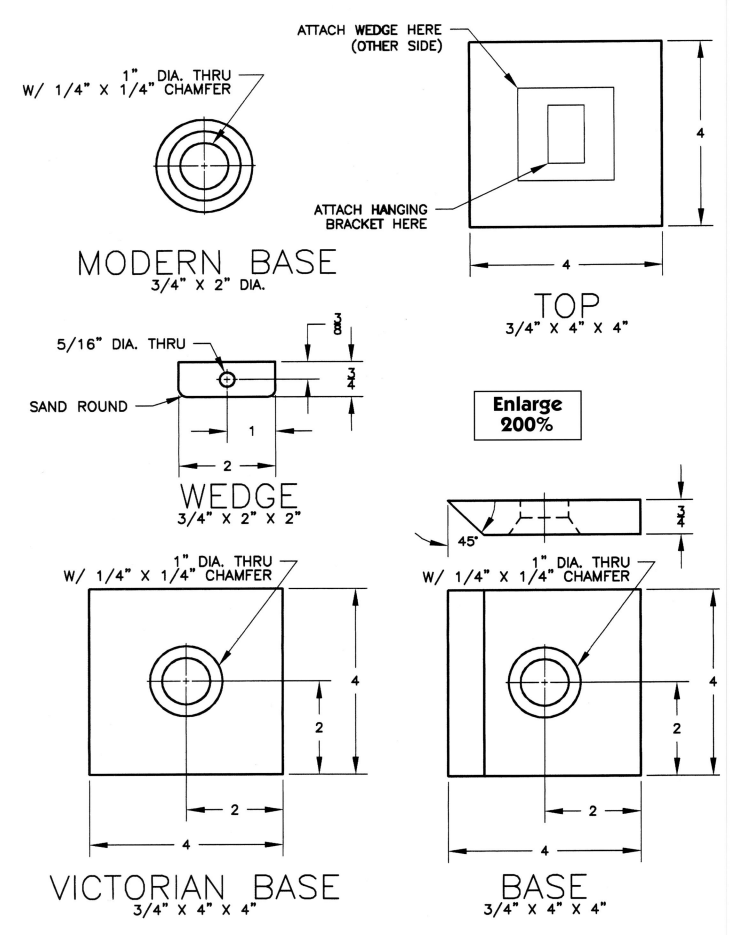

1" DIA. THRU
W/ 1/4" X 1/4" CHAMFER

MODERN BASE
3/4" X 2" DIA.

ATTACH WEDGE HERE
(OTHER SIDE)

ATTACH HANGING
BRACKET HERE

4

4

TOP
3/4" X 4" X 4"

5/16" DIA. THRU

SAND ROUND

3/8

3/4

1

2

WEDGE
3/4" X 2" X 2"

Enlarge
200%

45°

3/4

1" DIA. THRU
W/ 1/4" X 1/4" CHAMFER

4

2

2

4

1" DIA. THRU
W/ 1/4" X 1/4" CHAMFER

4

2

2

4

VICTORIAN BASE
3/4" X 4" X 4"

BASE
3/4" X 4" X 4"

THREE HUMMINGBIRD FEEDERS

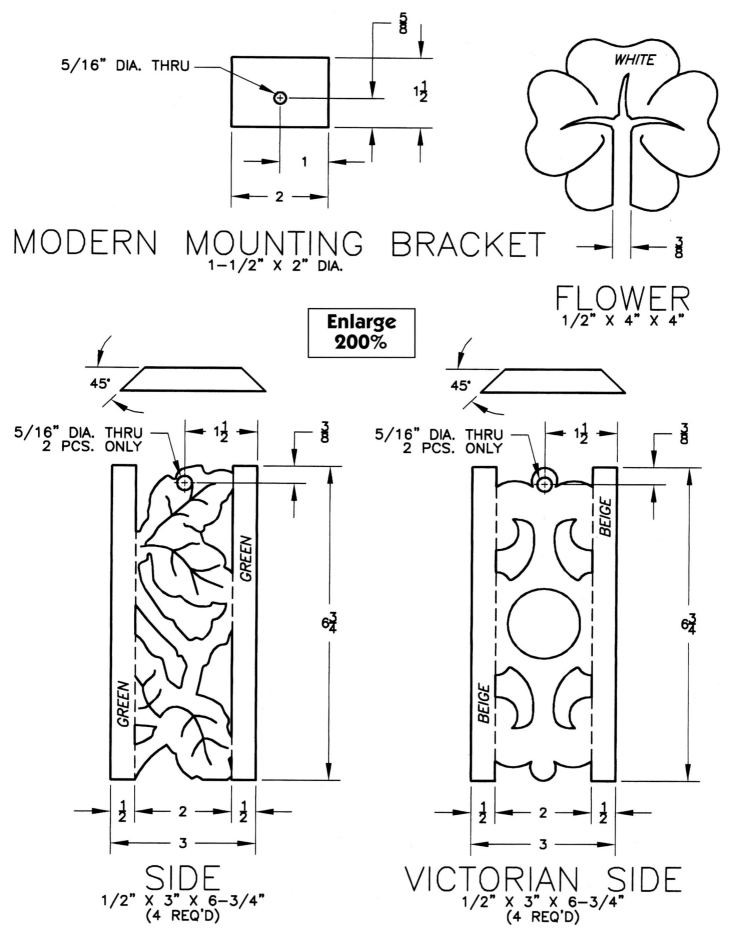

5/16" DIA. THRU

1

2

1½

5/16

MODERN MOUNTING BRACKET
1-1/2" X 2" DIA.

WHITE

3/16

FLOWER
1/2" X 4" X 4"

Enlarge 200%

45°

5/16" DIA. THRU
2 PCS. ONLY

1½

3/16

GREEN

GREEN

6¾

½   2   ½

3

SIDE
1/2" X 3" X 6-3/4"
(4 REQ'D)

45°

5/16" DIA. THRU
2 PCS. ONLY

1½

3/16

BEIGE

BEIGE

6¾

½   2   ½

3

VICTORIAN SIDE
1/2" X 3" X 6-3/4"
(4 REQ'D)

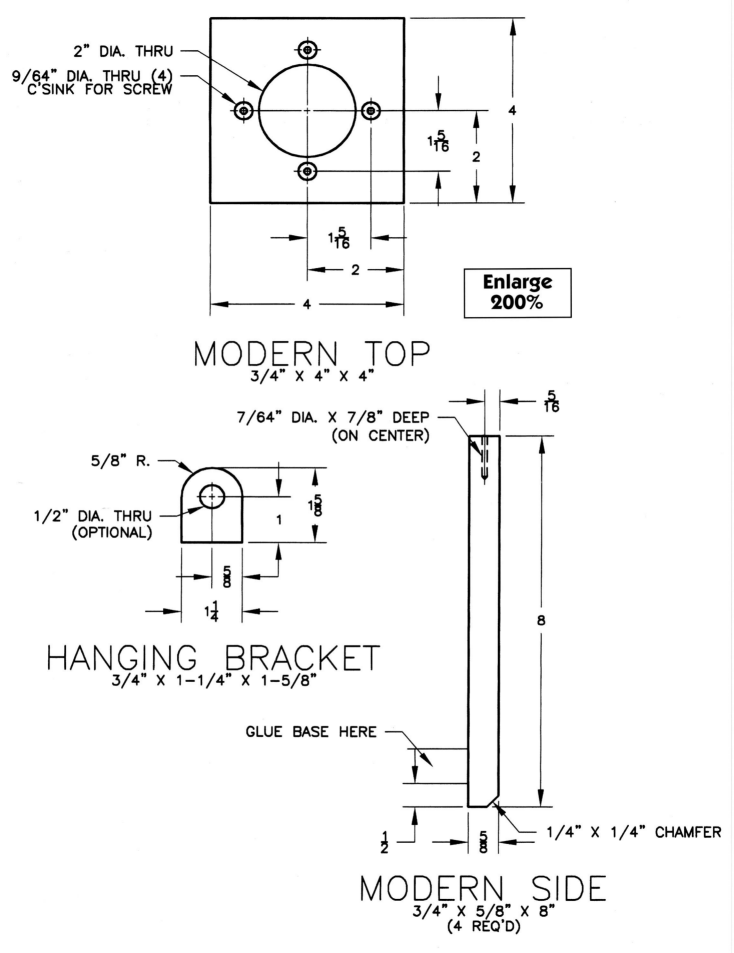

2" DIA. THRU

9/64" DIA. THRU (4)
C'SINK FOR SCREW

$1\frac{5}{16}$

4

2

$1\frac{5}{16}$

2

4

**Enlarge
200%**

MODERN TOP
3/4" X 4" X 4"

7/64" DIA. X 7/8" DEEP
(ON CENTER)

$\frac{5}{16}$

5/8" R.

1/2" DIA. THRU
(OPTIONAL)

$1\frac{5}{8}$

1

$\frac{5}{8}$

$1\frac{1}{4}$

8

HANGING BRACKET
3/4" X 1-1/4" X 1-5/8"

GLUE BASE HERE

$\frac{1}{2}$

$\frac{5}{8}$

1/4" X 1/4" CHAMFER

MODERN SIDE
3/4" X 5/8" X 8"
(4 REQ'D)

Hole Size Information

The following chart provides information on hole sizes and positions for several popular species. Additional information on other species is available through the many Internet sites devoted to birdfeeders and birdhouses or through your state's department of natural resources.

Species	Hole Size	Height above floor	Height off ground	Perch
House Wren	1⅛"	1"		No
Black-capped Chickadees	1⅛"	1½"	5-15'	No
White-breasted Nuthatches	1¼"	1"	12-20'	
Bluebird	1⅜" x 2¼" oval	1" (from top)	5-6'	No
Robin	(nesting shelf)		6-10'	
Eastern Phoebe (nesting shelf)				
Purple Martins	2¼"	1"	12-18'	
Northern Flicker	2½"	near top		
American Kestrel	3"	near top	10-30'	
Prothonotary Warbler	1⅛"	1"		
Pileated woodpecker	4"	near top		

Note: All entrances 1¼" in diameter or larger will admit house sparrows.

Feeding Preferences

East

Legend: ■ = Most Preferred ▨ = Preferred

Birds	Oil Sunflower	Hulled Sunflower	Striped Sunflower	Millet	Nyjer® (Thistle)	Cracked Corn	In-shell Peanuts	Shelled Peanuts	Suet	Safflower	Mealworms	Fruit	Nectar*
Perching Birds													
1. Bluebirds											■		
2. Cardinal, Northern	■	▨	▨							▨			
3. Chickadees	■	▨	▨					▨	▨		▨		
4. Finch, House	■	■	▨	▨	▨								
5. Finch, Purple	■	▨											
6. Goldfinches	▨	■			■								
7. Grosbeaks	■	▨	■								■		
8. Hummingbirds													■
9. Jays			▨				■	▨					
10. Nuthatches	■							▨	■				
11. Orioles											▨	■	■
12. Siskin, Pine	▨	■	▨		■								
13. Titmouse, Tufted								▨	■				
14. Woodpeckers		▨							■				
15. Wrens										▨	■		
Ground Feeding Birds													
16. Dove, Mourning	■			■		▨				▨			
17. Juncos	▨	▨		■		▨							
18. Sparrow, House	▨	▨		■		▨							
19. Sparrows, Native	▨	▨		■		▨							
20. Towhees				■		▨					■		

*Our own Pure Hummer Sugar™ • Nyjer® is a registered trademark of the Wild Bird Feeding Industry.

Courtesy of Wild Bird Centers of America, Inc.

West

Food Types

Birds	Oil Sunflower	Striped Sunflower	Hulled Sunflower	White Millet	Safflower	Nyjer® (Thistle)	Cracked Corn	Whole Peanuts	Shelled Peanuts	Suet	Mealworms	Fruit	Nectar*
Perching Birds													
1. Bluebirds											■		
2. Bushtit	□		□					■	□	■			
3. Chickadees	■	□	□							■	□		
4. Finches	■	■	□										
5. Flickers	□	□							□	■			
6. Goldfinches	□		■			■							
7. Grosbeaks	■	■											
8. Hummingbirds													■
9. Jays	□							■	■		□		
10. Kinglets			□							■			
11. Nuthatches	■	□							■	■			
12. Orioles												■	■
13. Siskin, Pine	□		■			■							
14. Titmouse	■	□	□		□				□	■			
15. Woodpeckers	■	□							■	■		□	
16. Wrens										□	■		
Ground Feeding Birds													
17. Doves	□		□	■			■	□					
18. Juncos								■					
19. Sparrows, Native	□		□	■				□					
20. Towhees				■									

Our own Pure Hummer Sugar™ • Nyjer is a registered trademark of the Wild Bird Feeding Industry.

Courtesy of Wild Bird Centers of America, Inc.

Appendix A

This Appendix is a source list for all specialty hardware and difficult-to-find supply items that are referenced throughout this book. Following the item description is the size and catalog part number. All parts can be ordered from the Meisel Hardware Specialties mail order catalog. (See reference at bottom of page.)

Description	Size	Meisel Part No.
Axle Pegs	5/32" x 5/8"	#AP6
Axle Pegs	11/32" Dia. x 2 3/8"	#AP5
Birdhouse Door	2" x 4 1/2"	#8606
Birdhouse Window	1 1/2" x 3 1/2"	#8607
Black Paint Marker	Fine Point	#3261
Carbon Paper	17" x 22"	#7347
Cedar Shakes	3/4" x 1 1/4"	#7688
Clear Acrylic Hopper Side	1/8" x 5 3/8" x 11"	#1377
Doll House Hinge	1/2" x 5/16"	#6510
Dowels	1/8" Dia. x 1 5/16"	#A35
Enjoying Purple Martins More Book	32 pages	#1294
Escutcheon Pin (For #6510)	1/8" x .023	#6509
Escutcheon Pin (For #8606 & 8607)	3/8" x #18	#388
Exterior Screws	1 1/4" x #6	#1455
Fiberglass Rod	3/8" Dia. x 36"	#8640
Finnish Birch Exterior Plywood	1/8" x 12" x 12"	#9981
Finnish Birch Exterior Plywood	1/4" x 12" x 12"	#9984
Finnish Birch Exterior Plywood	3/8" x 12" x 12"	#9985
Finnish Birch Exterior Plywood	1/2" x 12" x 12"	#9986
Finnish Birch Exterior Plywood	1/4" x 24" x 24"	#9705
Finnish Birch Exterior Plywood	3/8" x 24" x 24"	#9706
Finnish Birch Exterior Plywood	1/2" x 24" x 24"	#9878
Flush Mount Hanger	1 3/4"W x 1 1/2"H	#1262
Galley Spindle	1 1/8"	#S1
Gold Acrylic Paint	2 oz.	#02604
Half Round Dowel	3/8" x 3/4" x 16"	#8487
Hinge	1 1/2" x 1 1/2"	#1276
Hummingbird Feeder Hardware	6 1/2" bottles (pkg. of 3)	#1225
Jack Chain	#16	#9759
Perch Dowel (Multi-groove)	1/4" Dia. x 2"L	#1142
Polyurethane	1 pint	#9079
Sanding Sealer	1 pint	#9086
Screw	2" x #6	#1446
Screw Hole Buttons	3/8"	#1432
Screw Hole Buttons	7/8"	#1437
Screw Eye	5/16" Dia. x 13/16"	#2815
Screw Eye	5/8" Dia. x 1 9/16"	#3290
Spray Adhesive	11 oz.	#1447
Transfer Paper	18" x 24"	#9367
Treaded (Grooved) Wheels	2" Dia. x 3/4"W	#7050
Treaded (Grooved) Dual Wheels	2" Dia. x 1 1/2"W	#7051
Trim Head Finishing Screw	1 3/8" x #6	#6278
Water Resistant Glue	16 oz.	#3441
Wood Ball	3" Dia.	#1350
Wood Screw	1 1/4" x #8	#WS1148
Wood Screw	1 3/4" x #10	#WS13410

Available from Meisel Hardware Specialties. To request a catalog, write to Meisel Hardware Specialties, PO Box 70, Mound, MN 55364-0070 or call, 800-441-9870 or Visit Online, www.meiselwoodhobby.com

Appendix B

Full Size Pattern sheets can be ordered separately for each of the projects in this book. Order plans from Meisel Hardware Specialties 1-800-441-9870 or www.meiselwoodhobby.com. Be sure to use the part number below when placing your order.

Part #	Description
#W1698	Adirondack Birdhouse
#W541	Adobe Birdhouse
#W1881	American Home Birdhouse
#W542	Basement Birdhouse
#W1880	Country Church Birdhouse
#W1663	Country Cottage, Gardeners House, and Log Cabin Birdhouse
#W333	Martin House
#W544	Motor Home Birdhouse
#W1666	Nesting Shelf Birdhouse
#W543	Outhouse Birdhouse
#W861	Swinging Cat Birdhouse
#W1662	Three Easy Birdhouses
#W334	Tylorville Tudor Apartment Birdhouse
#W540	The White House Birdhouse
#W329	Wren Row Birdhouse
#W1699	Adirondack Birdfeeder
#W1673	Cardinal Birdfeeder
#W1654	Covered Bridge Birdfeeder
#W1672	Flutterby Birdfeeder
#W1655	Gazebo Birdfeeder
#W1451	Local Feed Supply
#W1661	Mallard Birdfeeder
#W1895	Sleeping Cat Birdfeeder
#W1545	Three Hummingbird Feeders

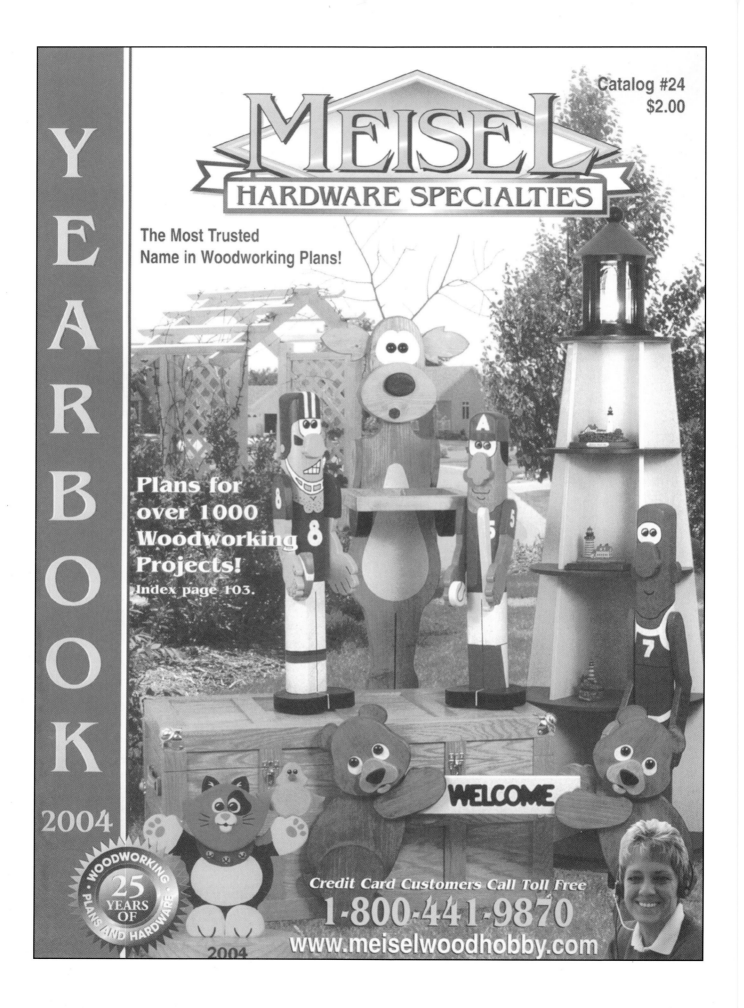

More Great Project Books from Fox Chapel Publishing

Birdhouse Builders Manual
By Charles Grodski and Roger Schroeder
Fill your backyard with practical and attractive birdhouses.
Includes four start-to-finish projects, measured drawings,
basic layout and wood information and more than 50
finished examples.
ISBN: 1-56523-100-7, 108 pages, soft cover, $19.95

Big Book of Christmas Scroll Saw Projects
By Paul Meisel
Any one of these 40-plus projects–including reindeer,
cardholders, Santa planters and more–will make a great
addition to your holiday decor. Includes complete material
lists, patterns and assembly plans for all pieces.
ISBN: 1-56523-185-6, 148 pages, soft cover, $17.95

Making Lawn Ornaments in Wood
By Paul Meisel
Stop traffic with these popular lawn and garden accessories.
Features complete instructions and patterns for thirty-four
projects and a full-color gallery and a paint mixing chart.
Detailed instructions cover choosing the wood, transfer-
ring, cutting and painting.
ISBN: 1-56523- 163-5, 72 pages, soft cover, $14.95

Woodworking Projects for Women
By Linda Hendry
One of America's most accomplished woodworkers, Linda
Hendry, guides other women step-by-step, through 15
Easy-to-Build Projects for the Home and Garden. The
book is designed to build your confidence, and has full-
color photographs and easy-to-follow instructions.
ISBN: 1-56523-247X, 72 pages, soft cover, $17.95

Violin Making
By Bruce Ossman
Make beautiful music with your own violin masterpiece.
The new, simplified process outlined here leads to great-
sounding results while using common woods and tools.
Features hundreds of detailed illustrations and full-size
patterns and templates.
ISBN: 1-56523-091-4, 67 pages, soft cover, $14.95

Easy-to-Build Bookcases and Clutter Control Projects
By The Editors of Weekend Woodcrafts
Build it. Use it. Use your woodworking skills to create
practical storage solutions for your home. From CD cases
and end tables to potting benches and more, you will find
projects to organize nearly every room of the house.
ISBN: 1-56523-248-8, 96 pages, soft cover, $17.95

Make Your Own Model Dinosaurs
By Danny A. Downs with Tom Knight
Everything you need to create exciting wooden dinosaur
models–just like the ones in the museum stores! Inside
you will find patterns and instructions for cutting and
assembling 7 different dinosaur projects. From the
tyrannosaurus to the velociraptor, you'll find patterns for
each and every dinosaur detail. Once all of the pieces are
cut, share the fun with your friends and family.
ISBN: 1-56523-079-5, 112 pages, soft cover, $17.95

Fireplace and Mantel Ideas, 2nd edition
By John Lewman
Design, build and install your dream fireplace mantel with
this updated edition of a popular classic. Inside you'll find
two new step-by-step instructions on carving a rustic mantel with woodcarving tools and building a classic fireplace
mantel using general woodworking skills and tools. In
addition, the author includes an amazing selection of classic
fireplace mantel designs including English traditional,
Country French, Victorian, Art Nouveau, and more.
ISBN: 1-56523-229-1, 196 pages, soft cover, $19.95

**Complete Guide to Making Wooden Clocks,
2nd edition**
By John A. Nelson
Nothing enhances a room's décor like a handsomely
crafted, hand-made wooden clock. Whether your passion is
stately grandfather clocks, timeless mantel clocks or modern desk clocks, you'll find all the information you need to
create your own timepiece.
ISBN: 1-56523-208-9, 184 pages, soft cover, $19.95

CHECK WITH YOUR LOCAL BOOK OR WOODWORKING STORE
Or call 800-457-9112 • Visit www.FoxChapelPublishing.com